TERMEDIATE
GUITAR METHOD

FINGERSTYLE

MW00666953

Approved Curriculum

The Complete Fingerstyle Guitar Method

LOU MANZI AND NAT GUNOD

Alfred, the leader in educational publishing, and the National Guitar Workshop, one of America's finest guitar schools, have joined forces to bring you the best, most progressive educational tools possible. We hope you will enjoy this book and encourage you to look for other fine products from Alfred and the National Guitar Workshop.

National Guitar Workshop Method
Approved Curriculum

Alfred Publishing Co., Inc.
16320 Roscoe Blvd., Suite 100
P.O. Box 10003
Van Nuys, CA 91410-0003
alfred.com

Copyright © MCMXCVIII by Alfred Publishing Co., Inc.
All rights reserved. Printed in USA.

ISBN-10: 0-7390-0594-4 (Book)
ISBN-13: 978-0-7390-0594-1 (Book)
ISBN-10: 0-7390-0595-2 (Book & CD)
ISBN-13: 978-0-7390-0595-8 (Book & CD)

Acquisition, editorial, internal design: Nathaniel Gunod, Workshop Arts
Music typesetting: Joe Bouchard, Workshop Arts
Photo acquisition: Michael Allain, Workshop Arts
CD performed by Lou Manzi
CD recorded and engineered at Bar None Studios in Cheshire, CT
Cover photo: Karen Miller

CONTENTS

ABOUT THE AUTHORS

Lou Manzi is the author of *Fingerstyle Guitar Technique Builder* and *Beginning Fingerstyle Guitar*, also published by Alfred and the National Guitar Workshop. He began his career in music in 1974 and has been on the faculty of the National Guitar Summer Workshop since 1984. He has performed extensively and teaches at the Tabor Community Arts Center in Guilford and Branford, Connecticut. Lou composed the all of the music in *Intermediate Fingerstyle Guitar,* and performed on the CD.

Nat Gunod is the chief editor for Workshop Arts, the publishing arm of the National Guitar Workshop. As of this writing, he has edited over 70 books and directed 10 videos. He is the author of *Classical Guitar for Beginners*, *Renaissance Duets: Play Along Library* and *Progressive Classical Solos*. Nat is an Associate Director of the National Guitar Summer Workshop (NGSW) and directs the NGSW Classical Guitar Seminar. He has performed all over the United States and taught students from all over the world at the Workshop and at various colleges, including the Peabody Conservatory of the Johns Hopkins University. He wrote all of the text for *Intermediate Fingerstyle Guitar*.

INTRODUCTION

Welcome to Intermediate Fingerstyle Guitar. You are reading this either because you have completed the first book in this series, *Beginning Fingerstyle Guitar*, or have determined that you are no longer a beginner, but you are not yet an advanced player. Go ahead and flip through the book you are holding...if you have all of this material down cold, you are probably a candidate for the last book in the series, *Mastering Fingerstyle Guitar*.

This book is for you if:

- You know how to read standard music notation and/or TAB
- You know the basic open chords and are ready to learn barre chords
- You have an understanding of basic theory (triads, major scale, diatonic harmony, key signatures, etc.) and are ready to learn 7th chord theory
- You play a number of different fingerpicking patterns, including Travis picking and are ready for more
- You know some basic altered tunings, such as Drop D and Open G and want to try more
- You are familiar with alternating bass lines and walking bass lines and want to learn about arpeggio bass lines
- You know techniques such as hammer-ons, pull-offs and natural harmonics and want to learn artificial harmonics, right hand slapping and right hand tapping.
- You want to begin learning how to arrange for fingerstyle guitar
- You want to study counterpoint
- You want to learn about the modes
- You want to play pieces in the styles of great fingerstyle players

Just in case you are starting *Intermediate Fingerstyle Guitar* without having gone through *Beginning Fingerstyle Guitar*, we have included plenty of review material in Chapter 1 and then as needed throughout the rest of the book. To get the most out of this or any other instruction book, practice the pieces slowly a section at a time. Remember, you can understand something intellectually almost immediately, but physically, it takes a lot longer. Be patient, keep an open mind, practice lots, and have fun!

A compact disc is available for this book. This disc can make learning with this book easier and more enjoyable. This symbol will appear next to every example that is on the CD. Use the CD to help insure that you are capturing the feel of the examples, interpreting the rhythms correctly, and so on. The track numbers below the symbols correspond directly to the example you want to hear. Track 1 will help you tune to the CD. Have fun!

CHAPTER 1

Review of the Basics

THE OPEN STRINGS

Holding your guitar in playing position, the strings are numbered from 6th to 1st with the 6th or lowest string being the one closest to the ceiling. Many beginning players don't know which end is up when it comes to the guitar. Since we are playing musical sounds, we refer to high and low depending upon the height and depth of our notes. The first string may be closest to the floor, but it is called the highest string because it is tuned to a higher *note* than the other strings. Music is made up of *notes*. A note is a musical sound, or *pitch*, of a specific degree of highness or lowness. Each note is given one of seven alphabetical names: A, B, C, D, E, F or G.

The following diagram shows that the strings are named E, A, D, G, B, E from 6th to 1st. The sentence "Ernie's Ant Does Get Big Eventually" may help you memorize these notes.

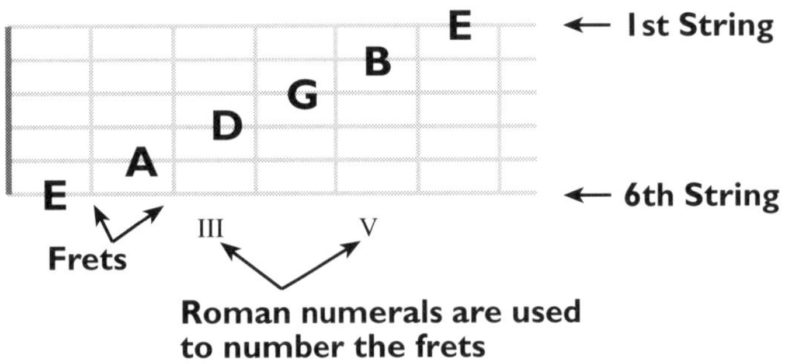

ROMAN NUMERALS

Here is a review of Roman numerals and their Arabic equivalents.

I ..... i 1	IV .. iv .. 4	VII ..... vii . 7	X .... x 10	XIII ... xiii ... 13	XVI ..... xvi 16
II ... ii ... 2	V ... v ... 5	VIII ... viii 8	XI ...... xi ... 11	XIV ... xiv ... 14	XVII .... xvii ... 17
III .. iii .. 3	VI .. vi .. 6	IX ...... ix ... 9	XII ..... xii . 12	XV .... xv 15	XVIII .. xviii .. 18

MUSIC NOTATION

Learning to read music on guitar is easy if you apply yourself and have some patience. You may not be able to rip through the Bach lute suites right away, but you'll get the basics covered quickly and, if you stick with it, you'll eventually be reading through more difficult pieces.

PITCH

Notes

Music is written by placing notes on a *staff*. Notes appear various ways.

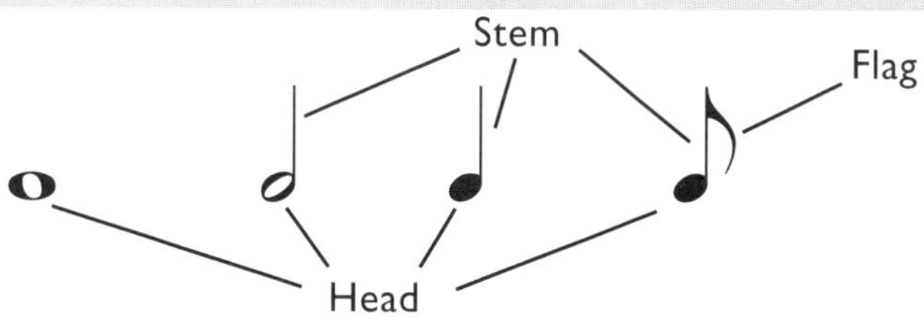

The Staff and Clef

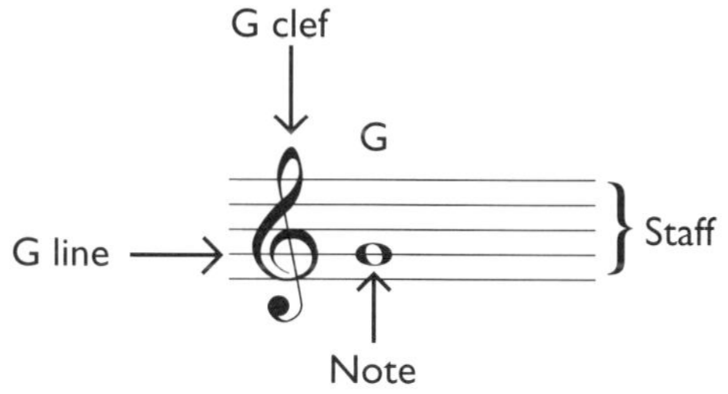

The staff has five lines and four spaces which are read from left to right. At the beginning of the staff is a *clef*. The clef dictates what notes correspond to a particular line or space on the staff. Guitar music is written in *treble clef* 𝄞 which is sometimes called the *G clef*. The ending curl of the clef circles the G line on the staff.

Here are the notes on the staff using the G clef:

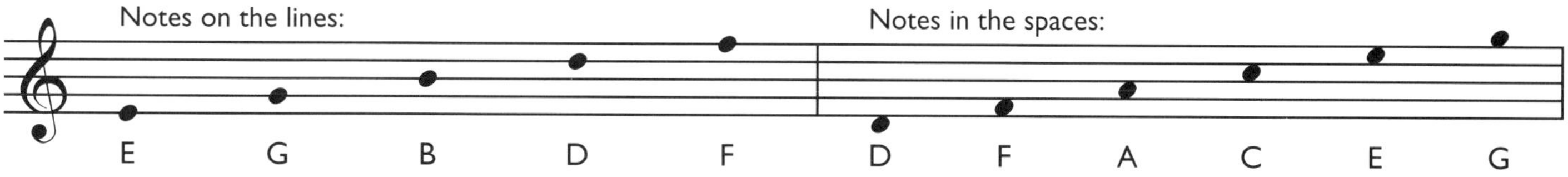

Ledger Lines

The higher a note appears on the staff, the higher it sounds. When a note is too high or too low to be written on the staff, *ledger lines* are used.

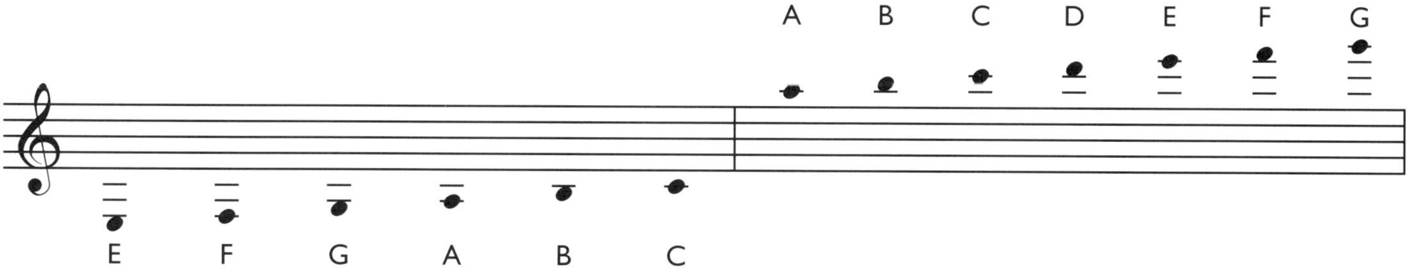

Guitar music is traditionally written one octave higher than it actually sounds. This allows us to write and read music on one clef, instead of using two clefs as with keyboard instruments.

Measures and Bar Lines

The staff is divided by vertical lines called *bar lines*. The space between two bar lines is called a *measure*. Measures divide music into groups of *beats*. A beat is an equal division of time. Beats are the basic pulse behind music. A *double bar* marks the end of a section or example.

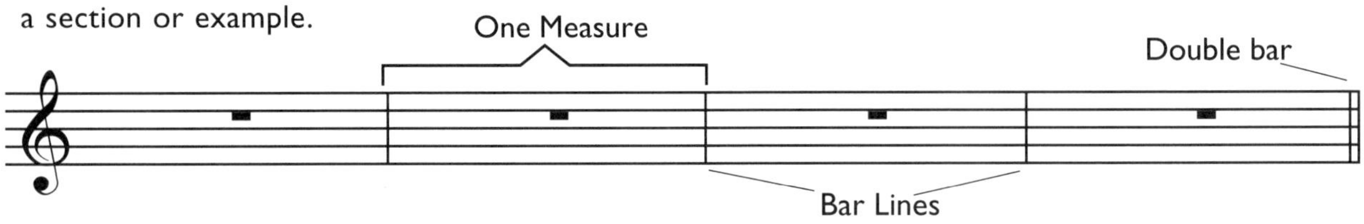

Note Values

As you know, the location of a note relative to the staff tells us its pitch (how high or how low it is). The duration, or value, is indicated by its shape.

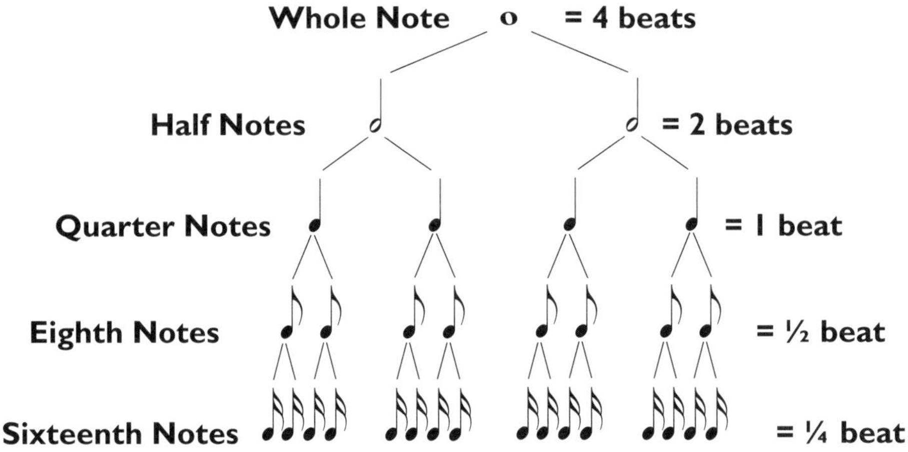

Time Signatures

Every piece of music has numbers at the beginning that tell us how to count time. The top number represents the number of beats per measure. The bottom number represents the type of note receiving one count.

4 ◄ 4 beats per measure
4 ◄ Quarter note ♩ = one beat

3 ◄ 3 beats per measure
4 ◄ Quarter note ♩ = one beat

6 ◄ 6 beats per measure
8 ◄ Eighth note ♪ = one beat

Sometimes a **C** is written in place of $\frac{4}{4}$. This is called *common time.*

Rest Values

Every note value has a corresponding rest. A rest indicates silence. A whole rest indicates four beats of silence, a half rest is two beats of silence, etc.

= Whole rest, 4 beats

= Half rest, 2 beats

= Quarter rest, one beat

= Eighth rest, ½ beat

= Sixteenth rest, ¼ beat

Ties

When notes are tied, the second note is not struck. Rather, its value is added to that of the first note. So, a half note tied to a quarter note would equal three beats.

= 3 beats

2 + 1

Notice the numbers under the staff in these examples. They indicate how to count. Both of these examples are in $\frac{4}{4}$ time, so we count four beats in each measure. When there are eighth notes, which are only ½ beat, we count "&" ("and") to show the division of the beats into two parts. When a counting number is in parentheses, a note is being held rather than struck.

Ties are a convenient way to notate notes that begin off the beat (on an "&").

1 2 & (3) & 4

Consecutive eighth notes are *beamed* together.

1 & (2) & (3) & 4

Dots

A dot increases the length of a note by one half of its original value. For instance, a half note equals two beats. Half of its value is one beat (a quarter note). So a dotted half note equals three beats (2 + 1 = 3). A dotted half note is equal to a half note tied to a quarter note.

1 + ½ 1½ 2 + 1 3 4 + 2 6

Dotted notes are especially important when the time signature is $\frac{3}{4}$ time, because the longest note value that will fit in a measure is a dotted half note. Also, dotted notes are very important in $\frac{6}{8}$ time, because not only is a dotted half note the longest possible note value, but a dotted quarter note is exactly half of a measure (counted 1 & ah 2 & ah).

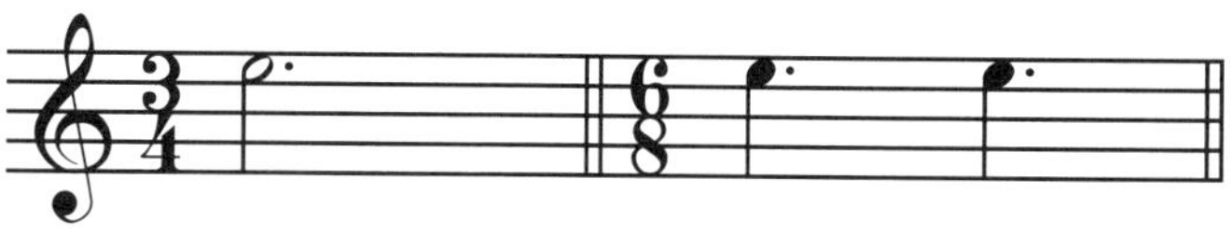

1 2 3 1 & ah 2 & ah

Triplets

A triplet is a group of three notes that divides a beat (or beats) into three equal parts.

Eighth-Note Triplet
(evenly divides one beat)

Quarter-Note Triplet
(evenly divides two beats)

Beaming

Notes that are less than one beat in duration are often beamed together. Notice the counting numbers: since there are four sixteenth notes in a beat, they are counted "1 e & ah 2 e & ah," etc.

Beamed eighth notes

Beamed sixteenth notes

The Right Hand Fingers
p = thumb
i = index
m = middle
a = ring
c = pinky

The Left Hand Fingers
1 = index
2 = middle
3 = ring
4 = pinky

Swing Eighths

In the blues and jazz styles, eighth notes are usually not played exactly as notated. Rather, they are interpreted in a "swing" style. This makes a pair of eighth notes sound like the first and last notes of a triplet.

Swing Eighths

Sound like this... ...but look like this.

Repeat Signs

These signs are used to indicate that music should be repeated.

Go back to the beginning and play these measures one more time.

Play the music between these signs twice.

Fingerstyle Notation

The standard rule in notation is that notes on the middle line of the staff or higher have their stems descending, and lower notes have their stems ascending. This won't work in lots of fingerstyle music, since it often involves playing more than one line at a time. In order to clearly separate the bass line when there is more than one line, we must borrow from classical guitar notation: we use descending stems for all notes played by the thumb, and ascending stems for all other pitches. This is an easy way to show two or more simultaneous melodic lines.

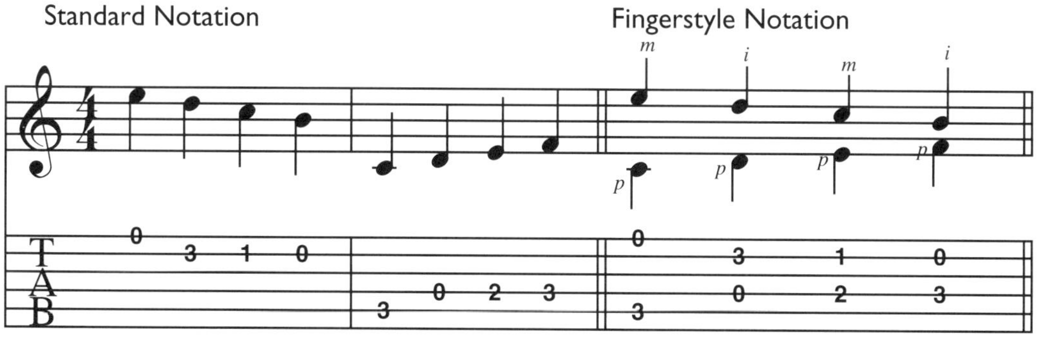

Scale Diagrams

The top line of a scale diagram represents the 1st (highest) string of the guitar, and the bottom line the 6th. The vertical lines represent frets, which are numbered with Roman numerals.

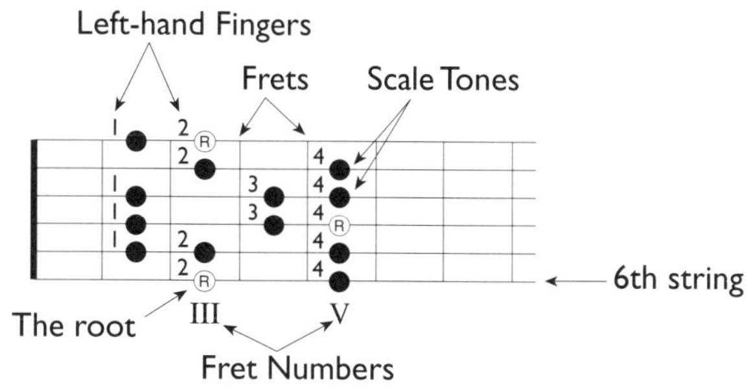

Chord Diagrams

Chord diagrams are similar to scale diagrams, except they are oriented vertically instead of horizontally. Vertical lines represent strings, and horizontal lines represent frets. Roman numerals are used to number the frets.

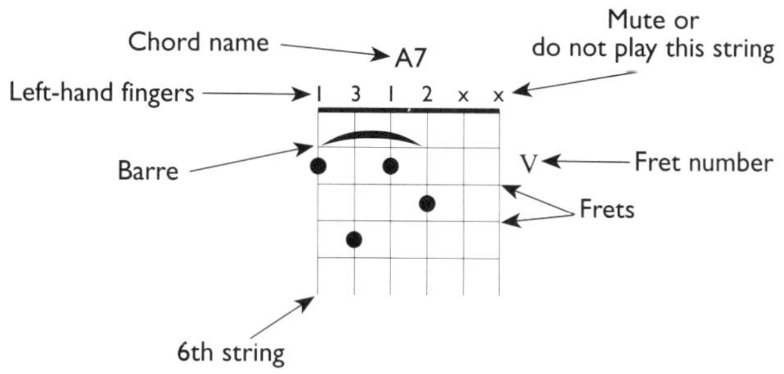

CHAPTER 2

Fingerstyle Patterns

REVIEW OF PATTERNS #1 - #11

Fingerstyle (or finger-picking) patterns are based on *chords*. A chord is any group of three or more notes (usually harmonious) played together. In fingerstyle guitar, we often play chords as *arpeggios*. In an arpeggio, the notes of a chord are played individually, rather than together. In this chapter you will be introduced to some basic right hand fingerstyle patterns. Although these easy arpeggios are often used for song accompaniments, creative composers also use them as the basis for their original instrumental pieces.

Notice the use of fingerstyle notation in these examples. The bass notes, played by the thumb of the right hand (*p*), are stemmed down, and the other notes are stemmed up. This makes it easier to find the bass line, and makes its independent identity as a separate part clear. Notice how many of the bass notes have two stems: one going up and one going down. This shows the bass line as distinct from the other notes, but also shows how it fits into the overall rhythm, usually as the first in a group of eighth notes.

1 #1

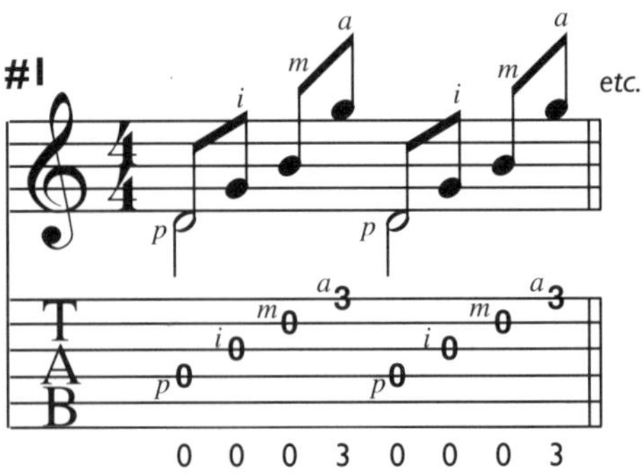

2 #2

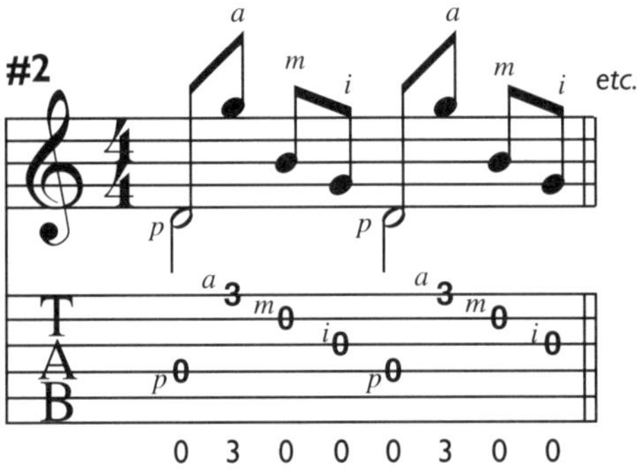

3 #3

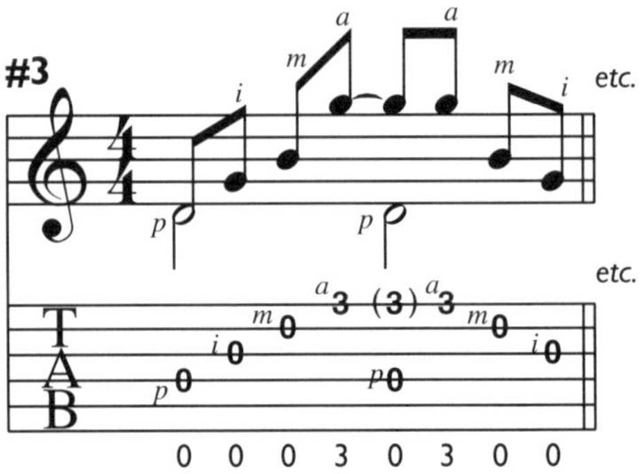

4 #4

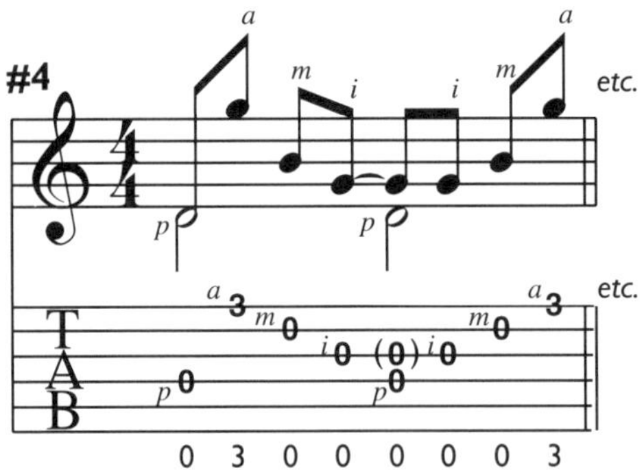

5 #5

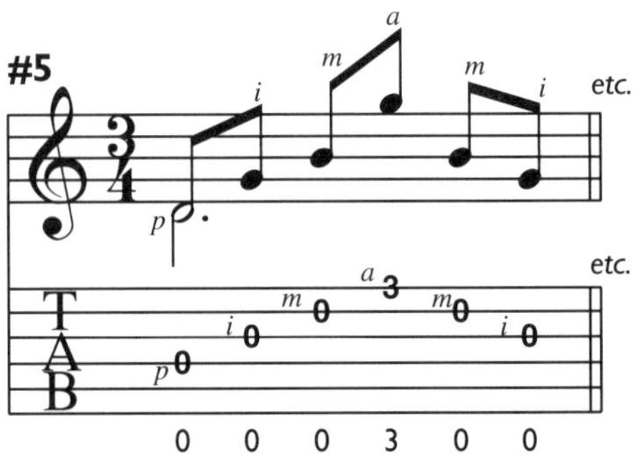

6 #6

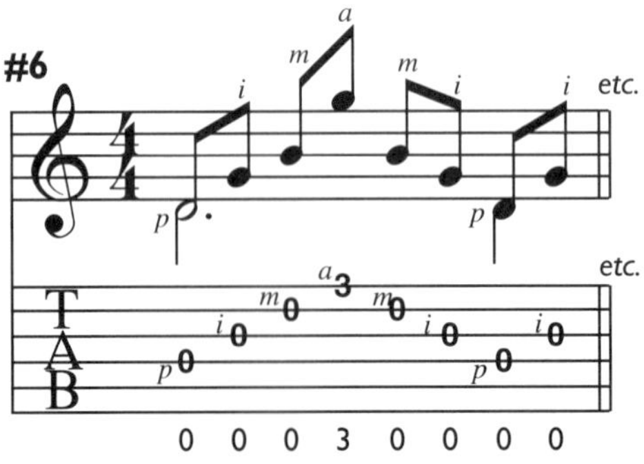

7

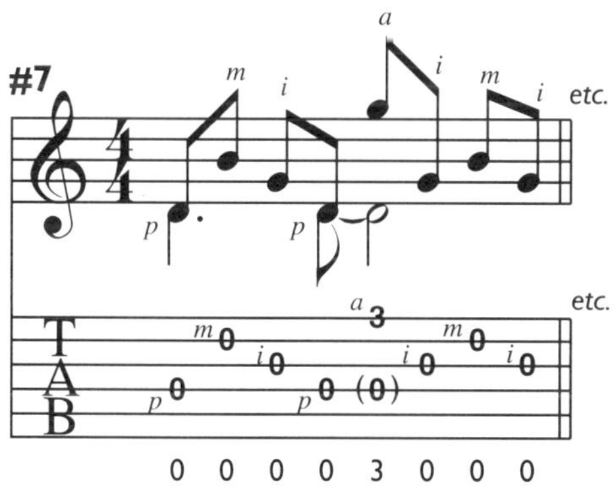

8

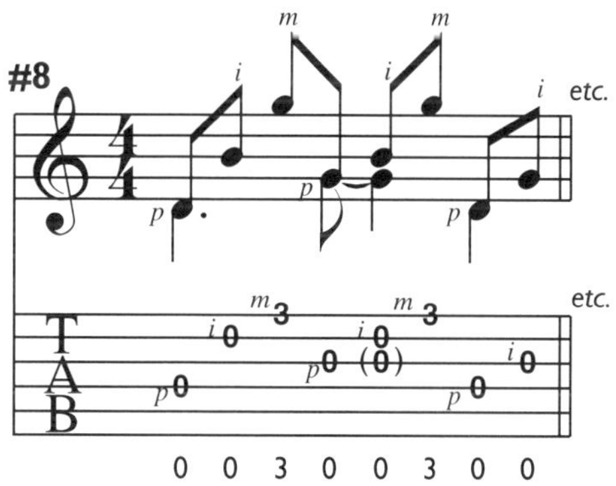

9

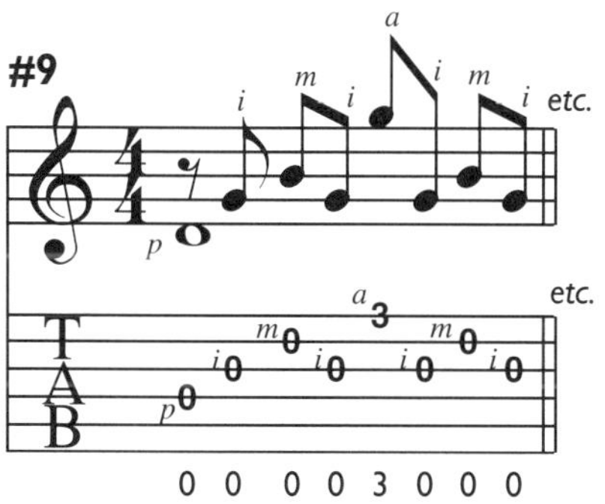

10

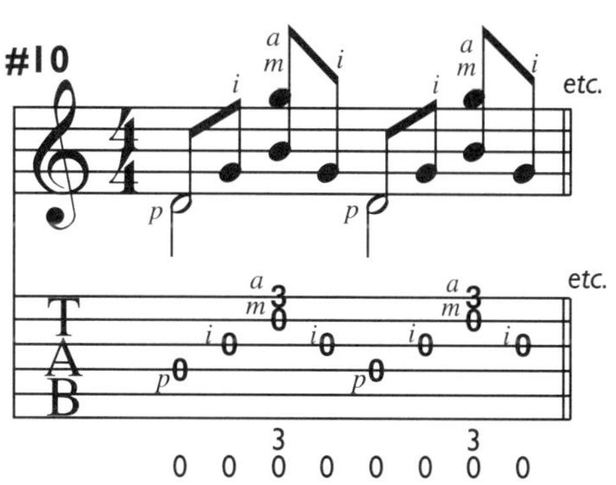

11

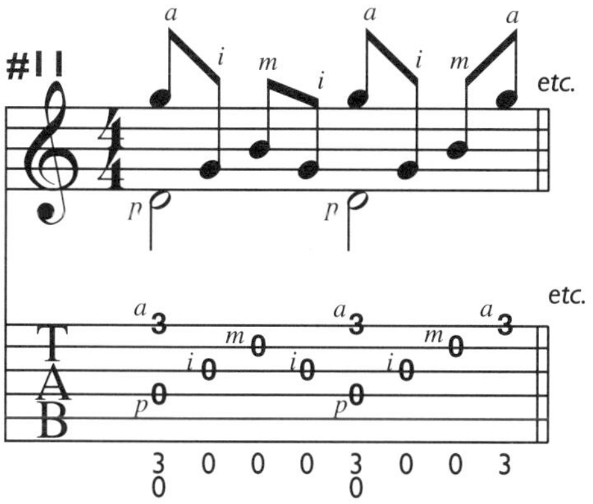

PATTERN #12

Pattern #12 creates a new pattern with a part of pattern #10: the double stop with *m* and *a* followed by a single note with the *i* finger. In this case, *p* is combined with the double stop. As *p*, *m* and *a* play, release *i* to its strings. As *i* plays, re-extend *p*, *m* and *a*. Continue alternating in this way.

12

Track 2

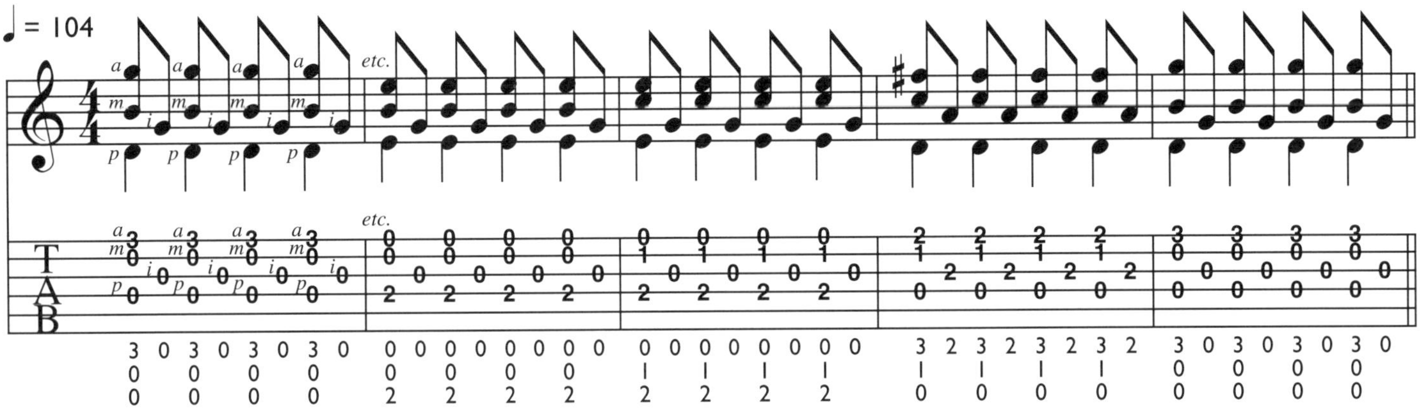

Example 13 will give you more practice with Pattern #12.

13

Track 3

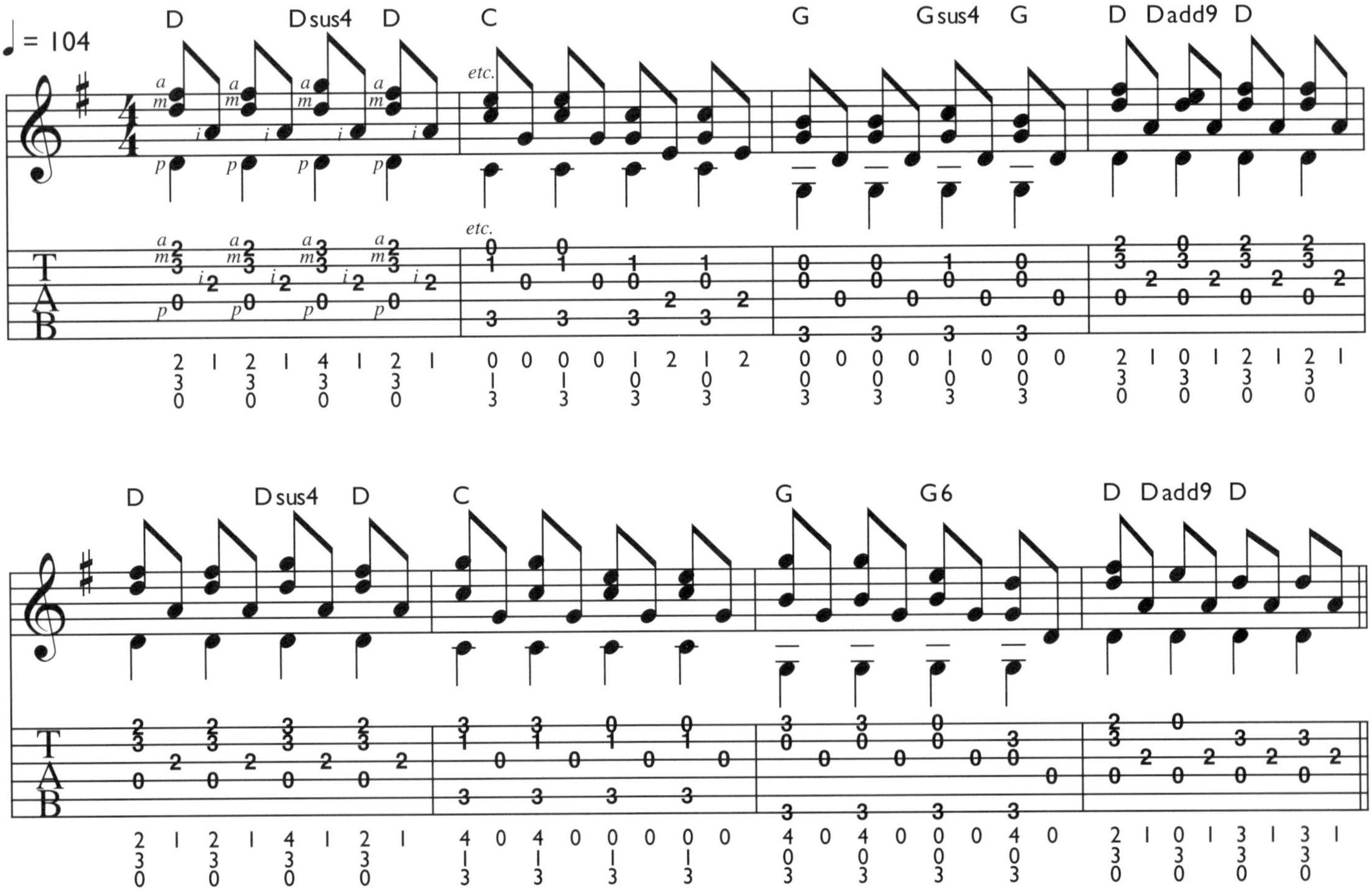

PATTERN #13

Pattern #13 is based on the same Latin (South American) rhythm as Pattern #8. This time, the rhythm is even more pronounced because *a* and *p* play together, further emphasizing the 1-2-3, 1-2-3, 1-2 rhythm of the bass. Start with *a*, *m* and *i* all poised to play their respective strings. The fingers should follow each other into the hand, and as *i* plays *a* and *m* should release back their strings. Return *i* back to the 3rd string as *a* strokes the 1st. Always return *p* to its string as *a* returns to the 1st string. On the last eighth of each measure, return *a* to the 1st string as *m* plays.

14

Track 4

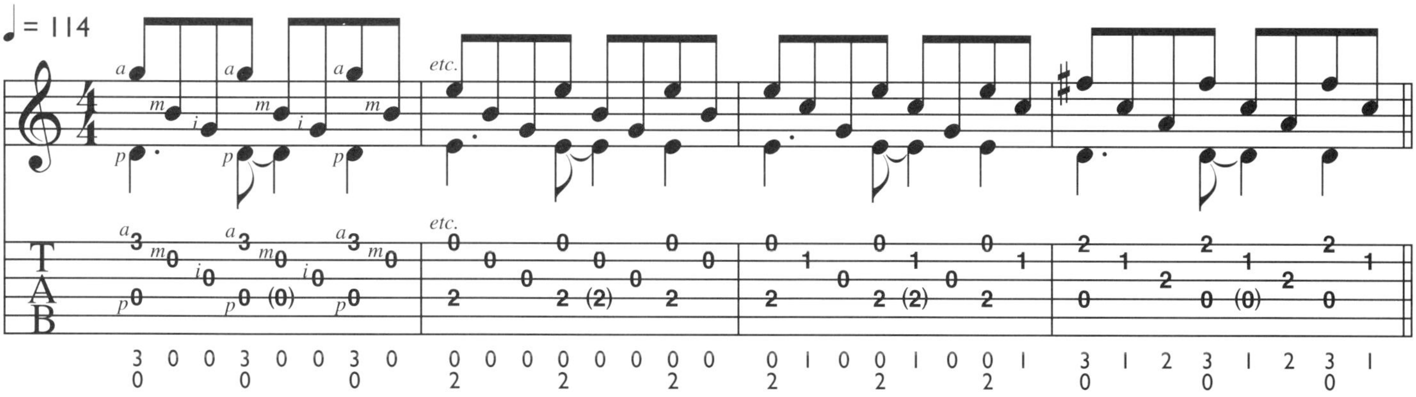

Enjoy playing this example based on Pattern #13.

15

Track 5

PATTERN #14

Pattern #14 is based on the alternating bass Travis picking introduced in Chapter 8 of *Beginning Fingerstyle Guitar*. The *p* finger alternates between the 6th and the 4th or the 5th and the 4th strings. Try to move *p* from the wrist joint, where the thumb connects to the wrist. Keep the hand stilll as you keep the steady quarter note rhythm of the bass going. There is plenty of time to prepare *m* on the 1st string before playing. This will give you added security and control of the tone.

16

Track 6

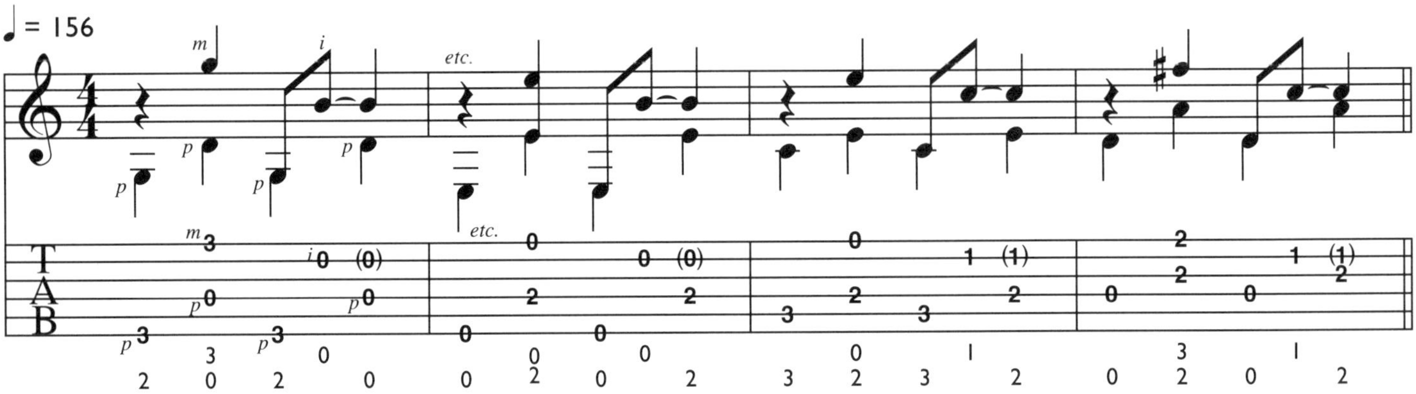

Remember, slash chords such as the D/F♯ in the second measure of Example 17 indicate the chord shown has a note other than the root in the bass. For instance, D/F♯ indicates a D Major chord with an F# in the bass.

17

Track 7

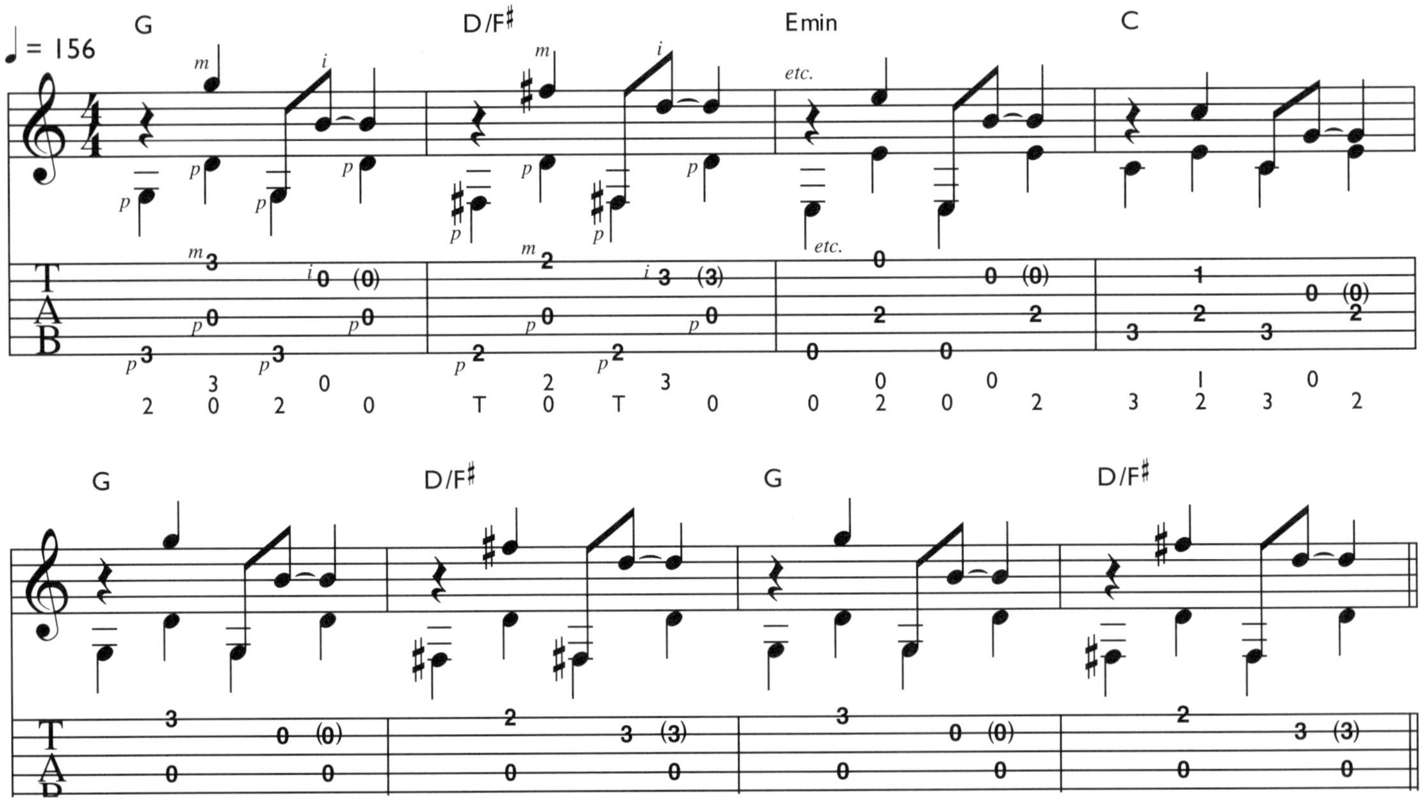

PATTERN #15

Another variation on Travis picking, Pattern #15 provides another opportunity to practice finger alternations (this time between *i* and *m*) against a steady, driving alternating bass. Remember to keep your hand as still as possible. Let your fingers do the work!

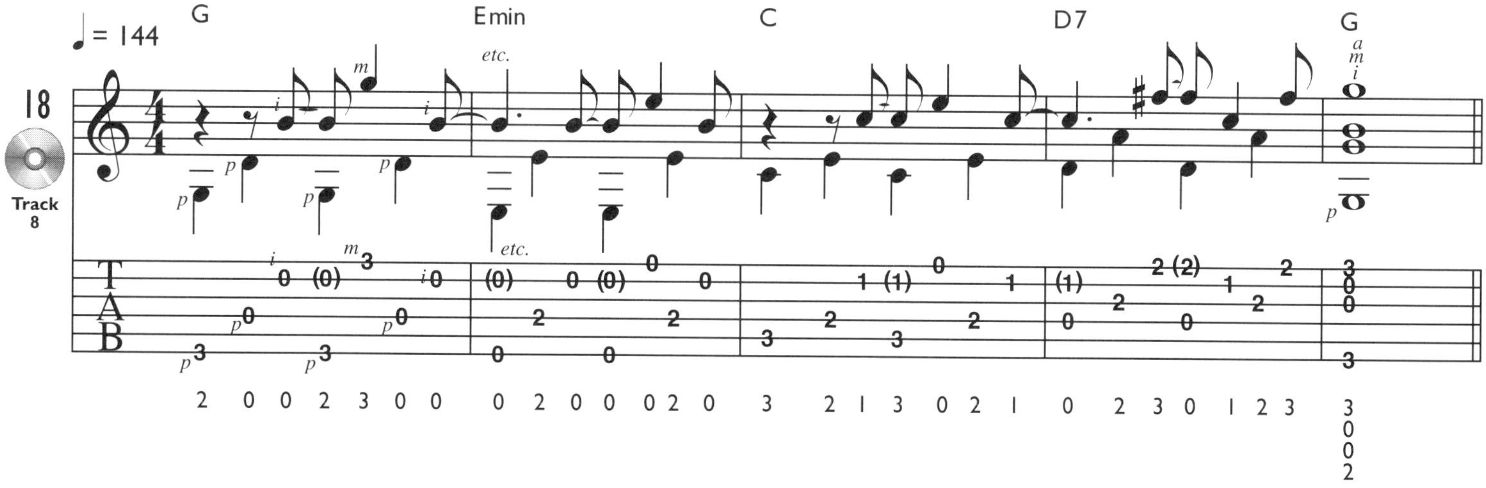

Example 19 is chock-full of new and interesting chords. Spend some time with each and get to know their sounds. Here they are:

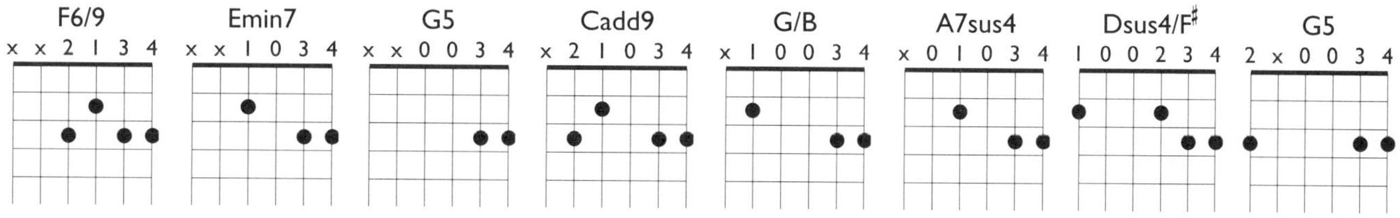

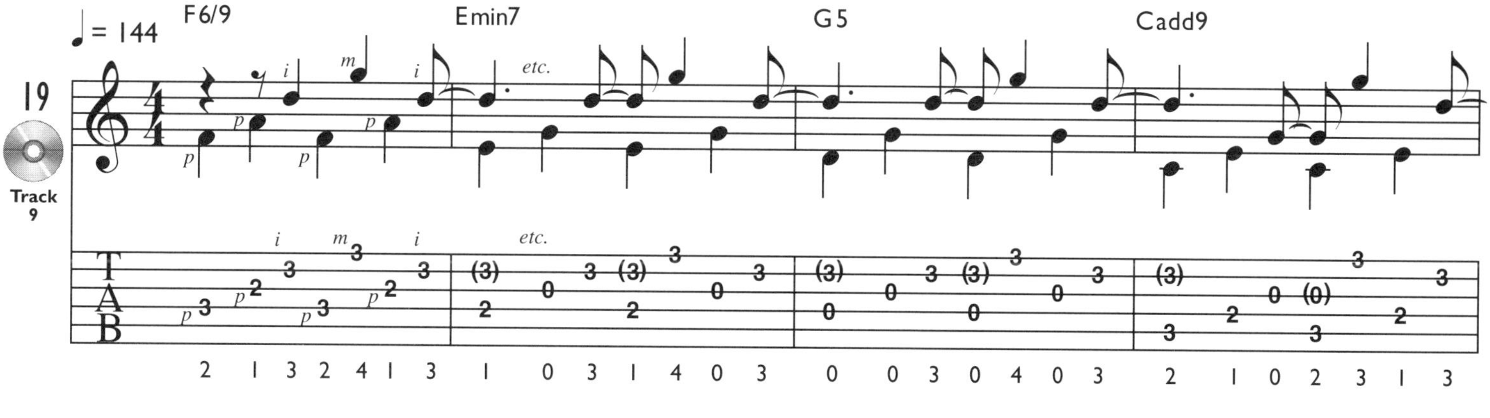

CHAPTER 3

Special Techniques

MULTIPLE HAMMER-ONS AND PULL-OFFS

By now, you are probably well acquainted with *hammer-ons* and *pull-offs*. If not, it would be a good idea to study Chapter 11, starting on page 68 of *Beginning Fingerstyle Guitar*.

Briefly, hammer-ons and pull-offs, otherwise known as *slurs*, are the most commonly used devices for creating *legato* (smooth) connections between notes on the guitar. In both techniques, the right hand plucks the first note and subsequent notes are played by the left hand. Slurs are notated with a slur sign ⁀ and an H for hammer-ons, or a P for pull-offs.

In this section, we will be expanding on these techniques connecting more than two notes with hammer-ons and pull-offs. That's right...you can play more than two notes with only one pluck. This is a great way to group notes together and play quickly. While it is very important to learn to pluck rapidly, there's no harm in getting a little speed with less effort. And, as long the notes involved can be played on a single string, hammer-ons and pull-offs can get you three or more very quick notes for the price of one!

As always, an important issue with these legato techniques is rhythm. It is challenging to build a technique that can perform rhythmically even hammer-ons and pull-offs. Beware of the tendency to rush into the second or third notes in, say, a three note group. Practice your eight-note slurs with a metronome set to eighth notes. This will help you acquire a feel for even legatos.

The next three pages contain examples and pieces using these techniques. Practice them all slowly at first, with a metronome. Have fun!

PHOTO COURTESY OF GAMI-SIMMONS

One of the few classical guitarists to successfully cross-over into the fingerstyle "acoustic music" world, **Benjamin Verdery** *came to prominence in the 1980s. He has performed to delighted audiences in both fingerstyle and classical guitar festivals all over the world. Check out his* Some Towns and Cities, *also published by the National Guitar Workshop and Alfred.*

Check it out! By measure three of Example 20, you'll be whippin' out those sixteenth note licks like butter. Work-up to playing them quickly—practice somewhat slowly at first. You will find that it is impractical to practice hammer-ons and pull-offs *too* slowly. At very slow speeds, rhythmic accuracy becomes unreasonable to expect.

Pay special attention to the last note in the first measure (D on the 2nd string). This note is played with a hammer-on, even though the string has yet to be struck by the right hand. In a way, this is really a *tap*. Make sure that the 2nd finger strikes the 3rd fret with sufficient force to make the D note sound clearly, but not so much that the note sounds percussive.

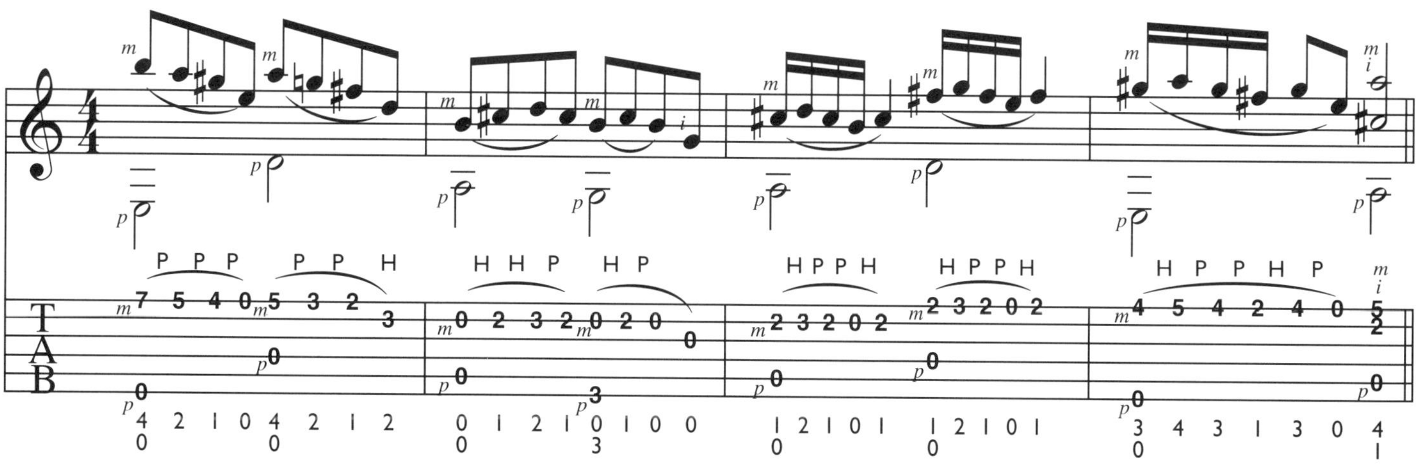

Example 21 introduces double-stop hammer-ons and pull-offs. There is nothing really new here, although it may feel new. In hammer-ons, make sure you are lifting and dropping both fingers together. In pull-offs, take care to pull both fingers off together. In both cases, strive to maintain a good balance between the parts--the upper and lower notes in each double-stop should sound at the same volume.

21

Track 11

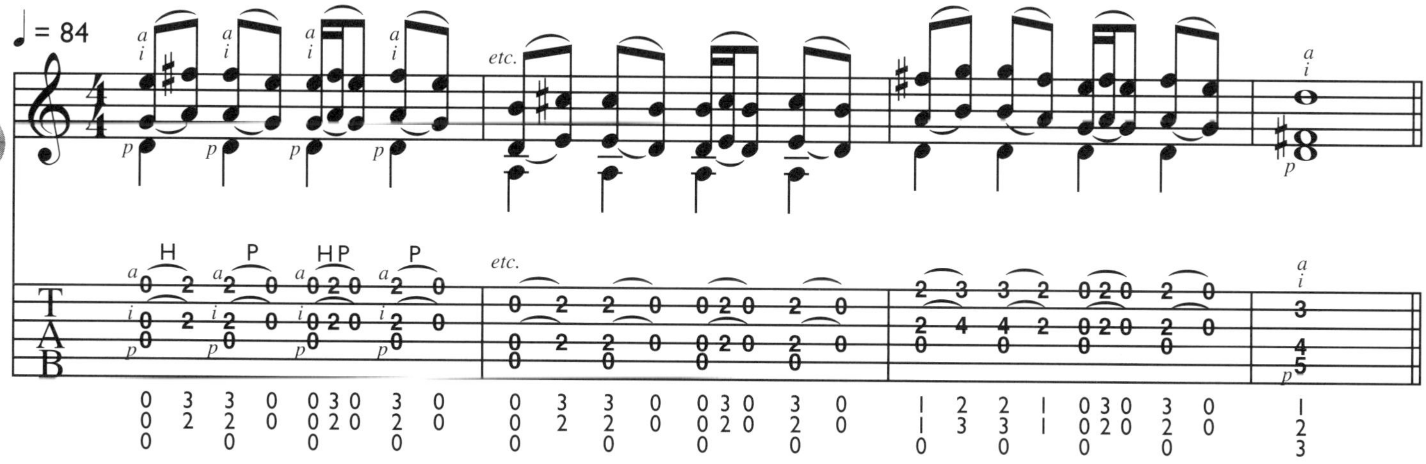

DESERT RIDE

Track 12

Tune your 6th string down to D for this one.

NIGHT OUT

Track
13

ARTIFICIAL HARMONICS

By now, you have certainly listened to lots of guitar music. You may have noticed occasional high chiming notes that have a bell-like tone. These were probably *harmonics*. Every musical note, or *fundamental tone*, is accompanied by an array of *overtones*. We aren't usually aware of them--they are just there, the way that many colors of the spectrum are there when we perceive a specific color. A harmonic is what happens when we touch the string in such a way as to isolate one of these overtones from the fundamental tone and most of the other overtones. These high, pure sounding tones are distinctive, and add a beautiful color to pieces. They can be very effective as highlights in the music. There are various ways to make harmonics on the guitar. In *Beginning Fingerstyle Guitar*, page 74, we covered natural harmonics. Now, it's time to discuss *artificial harmonics*.

While natural harmonics are made by touching the string lightly at certain points on the string with the left hand (the 12th, 7th and 5th frets are most common), artificial harmonics involve a different technique. Here is how to perform an artificial harmonic that sounds an octave higher than the fundamental tone:

- Finger the desired note normally with the left hand.
- With the *i* finger of the right hand, lightly touch the same string directly over a fret exactly twelve frets higher than the fingered note. For instance, if the fingered note is one the 1st fret, touch a spot directly over the 13th fret with the right hand.
- While touching the string with *i*, pluck the string with *p* or *a*.
- Immediately upon striking the note, quickly lift the right hand away from the string, allowing it to ring clearly.

Experiment with this for a little while. Remember that as you change from note to note, the right hand will mirror the motion of the left-hand fingers. As you finger higher notes on a string, your right hand will move to the right. As you finger lower notes on a string, your right hand will move to the left. Work on the timing between plucking the string with *p* or *a* and lifting your right hand away from the strings so that the notes ring clearly. Notice the diamond shaped noteheads in the example below, indicating harmonics. Unless marked otherwise, all of the artificial harmonics are as described above—twelve frets higher than the fingered note.

In Examples 22 and 23, pluck with *p*.

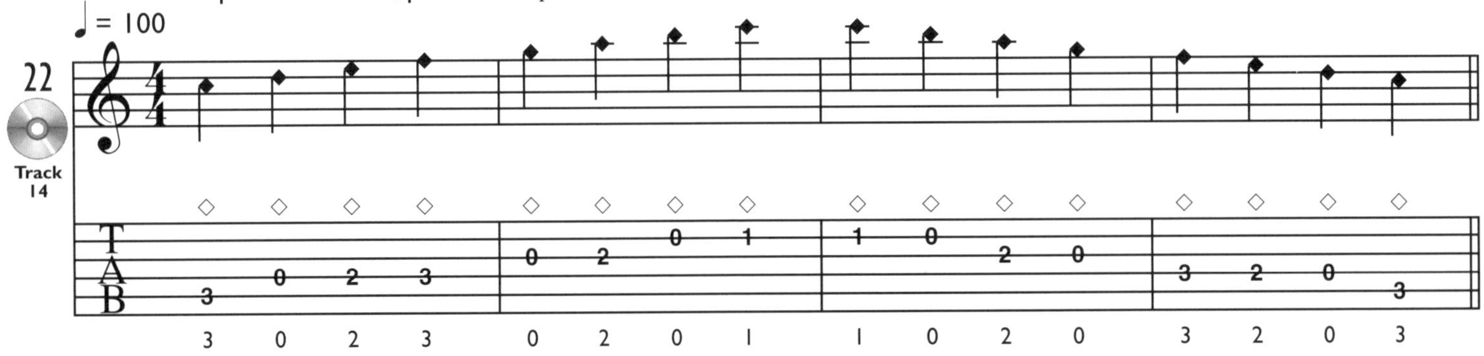

23

Track 15

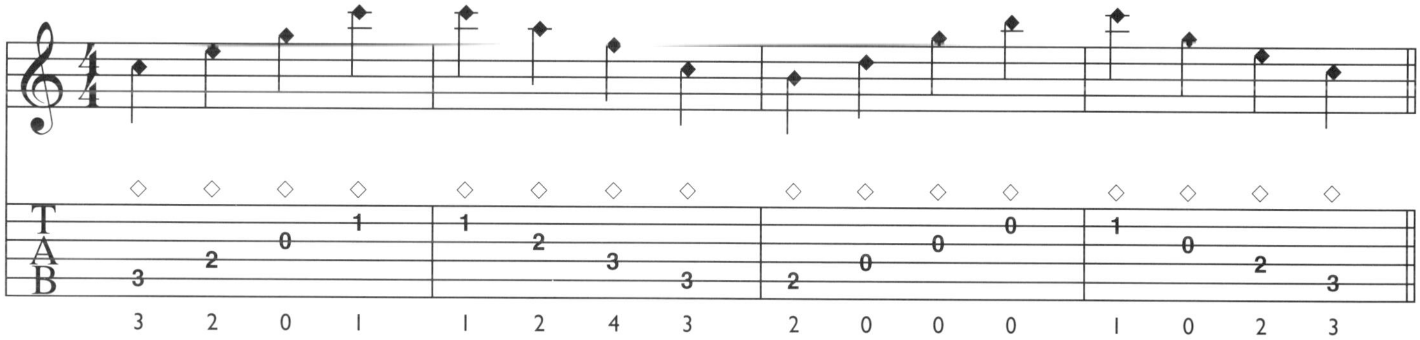

In Example 24, artificial harmonics are mixed in with normal notes. Since the artificial harmonics are fingered on the lower strings, continue to pluck them with *p*. But here's something you may never have tried before: pluck the normal notes with your pinky (*c*)! Yes, this will take some getting-used-to, but it works out well because your right hand will be tilted towards the pinky so that *p* can pluck the harmonics. Have fun.

24

Track 16

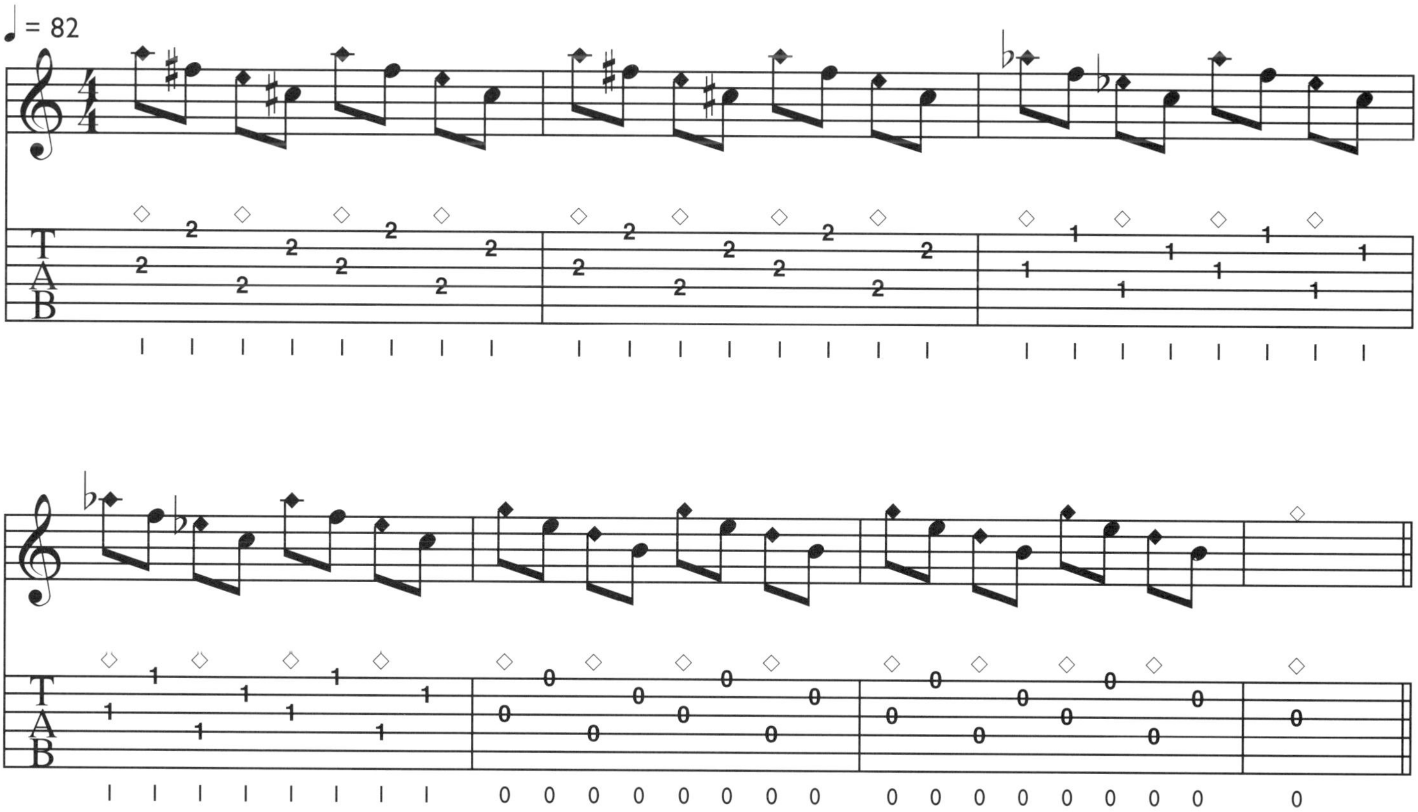

PHOTO\CLAUDIO CORRIVETTI\COURTESY OF ROUNDER RECORDS

French-Algerian guitarist ***Pierre Bensusan*** *became known in the 1980s. His highly expressive and exotic playing have made him one of today's most influential players.* *See pages 48 - 51 of this book to learn about his unque style.*

Now it's time to try plucking artificial harmonics with the *a* finger. Continue to use *i* to lightly touch the strings above the desired frets. This technique is usually used when the harmonics are played on the upper three strings. Learn the harmonics in Example 25 before putting them together with the bass notes, which are played with *p*.

25

Track 17

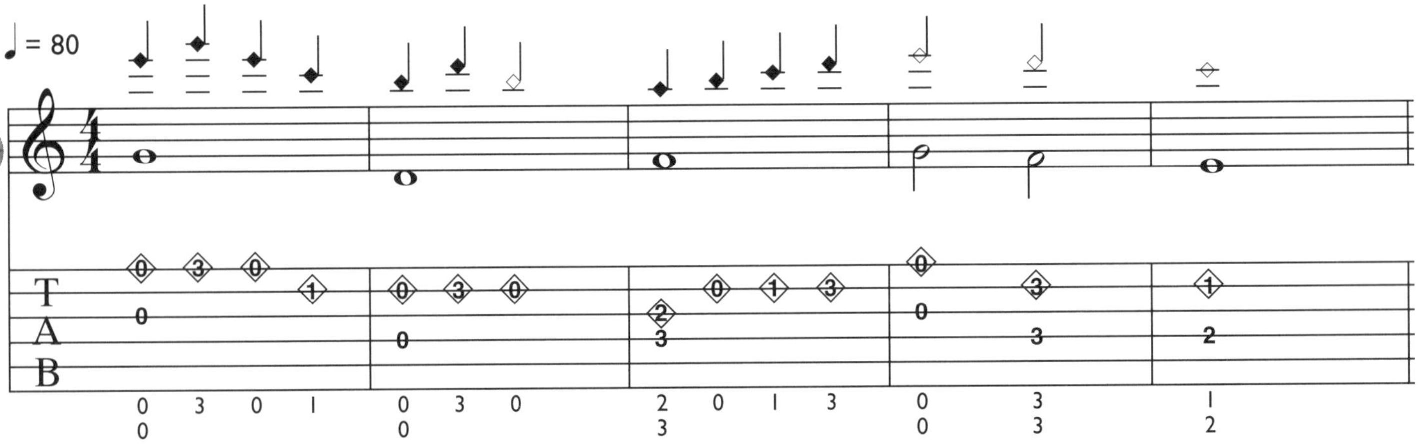

Here is yet another artificial harmonics technique. Pluck the normal notes (stems down) with your pinky, and pluck the harmonics (stems up) with *p*!

26

Track 18

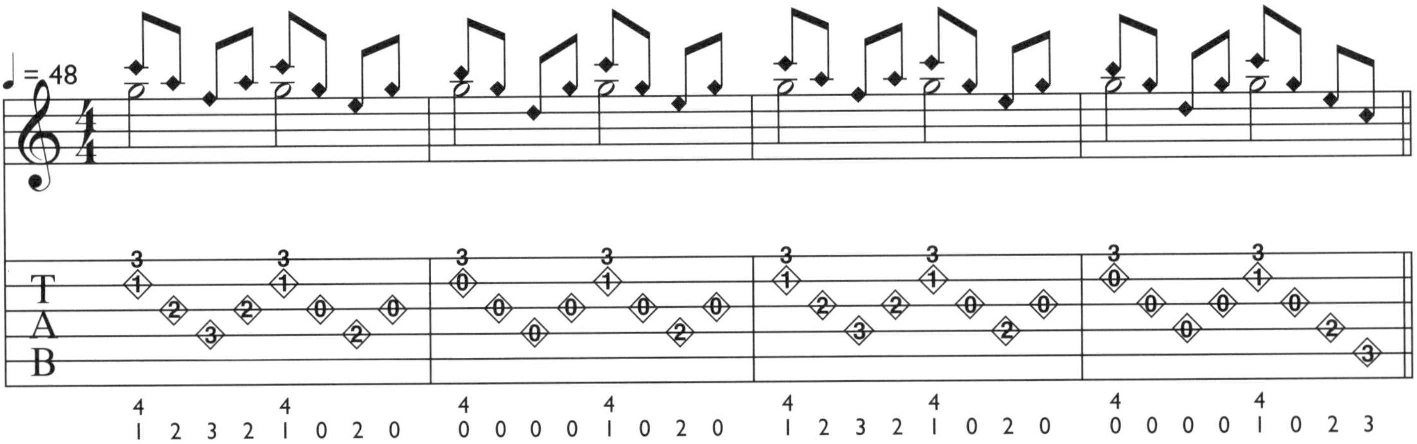

In the following piece, play all the harmonics with *i* and *p*. All other notes should be plucked with your pinky.

STAR CATCHER

Track 19

CHAPTER 4

Barre Chords

THE TECHNIQUE

Barre chords are an essential technique for all guitarists. The most important feature of barre chords is that they contain no open strings. This simple fact makes these chords indispensable because, since they contain no open strings, they can be played in any key anywhere on the neck.

To perform a barre, lay your 1st finger across all six strings just to the left of the fret. For now, try this on the 5th fret. Pull your left elbow in towards your side slightly. This will help you to use the thumb side of the 1st finger, thus avoiding the indentations at the joints of the finger, increasing your leverage and making it easier to use the other fingers. Try to use just enough strength to allow all six strings to ring clearly when plucked. Try to keep the 1st finger fairly straight—parallel to the fret. Slowly pluck all six strings. If one string doesn't ring clearly, try adjusting your left hand up (towards the ceiling) or down (towards the floor) to put slightly more or slightly less finger over the neck. Make sure you have your left elbow in closer to your side than normal. We all have different sized hands and need to experiment to find the right position for each barre.

Another important variable in playing barre chords is, believe it or not, your guitar. Some guitars have a "low action," where the strings are very close to the frets and easy to push down. Some guitars have a "high action," and are more difficult to play. While barre chords require a bit more strength than other notes and chords, if you are using your elbow, hand and finger positions to their best advantage, they shouldn't require *that* much strength. If you find barres unreasonably difficult to play even after considering all the technical variables, maybe you should have your action adjusted down or consider a lighter set of strings.

Another important variable for playing barre chords is the number of strings being barred. For instance, if you are playing a chord where the 6th, 2nd and 1st strings are barred and the other strings are taken with other fingers, your barre need only work on the three barred strings. You can work on controlling which part of the 1st finger works the hardest.

ROOT 6 AND ROOT 5 BARRES

The two most common types of barre chord are the root 6 and root 5 barres. As you know, every chord has a root. Root 6 barres have their roots on the 6th string, root 5 barres have their roots on the 5th string. The neat thing is, if you know all the names of the notes on these two strings, you can play any barre on any root. A♭ Minor? No problem, just find an A♭ on the 6th or 5th string and play the appropriate barre chord!

As you will notice when studying the chart on page 27, the root 6 chords are based on the open position E chords, and the root 5 chords are based on open position A chords. Check it out! Make sure you memorize and master all the chords on the chart. Have fun.

ROOT 6 BARRES

Major

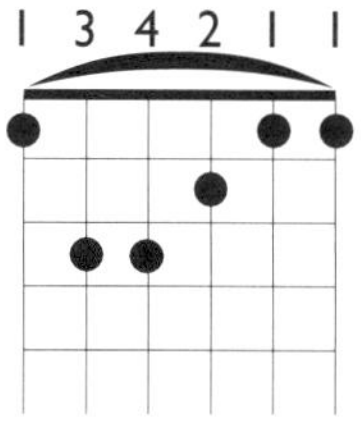

Minor

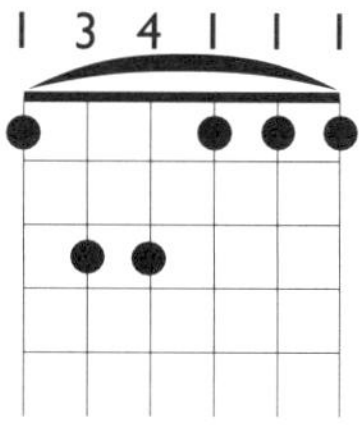

7th

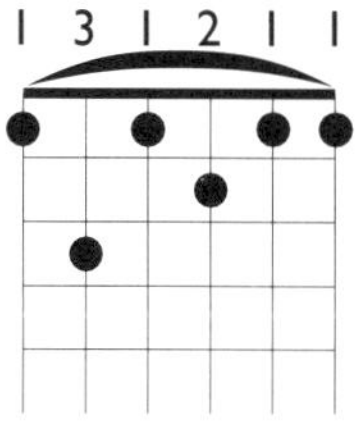

7th

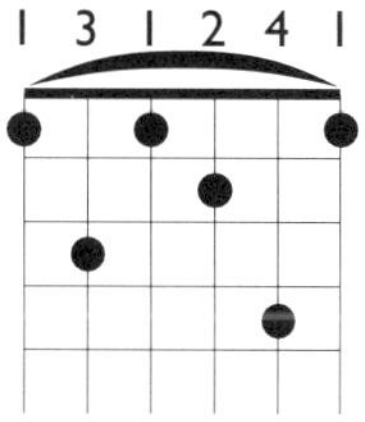

ROOT 5 BARRES

Major

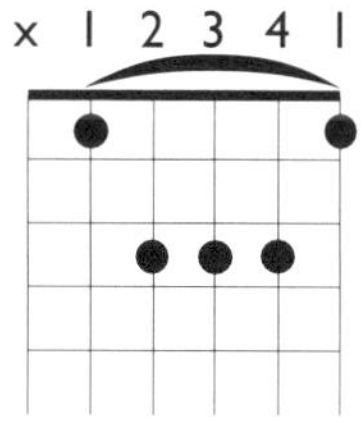

Major

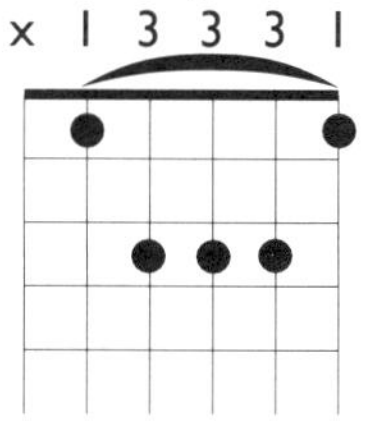

(Alternate Fingerings)

Major

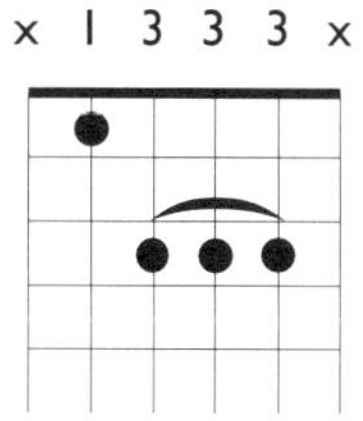

Major

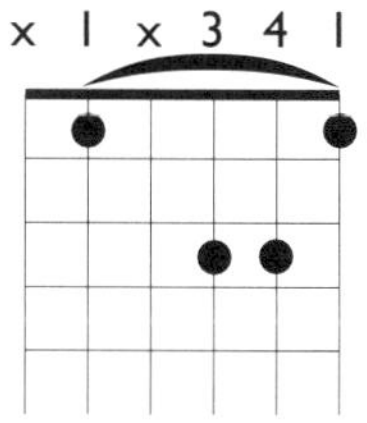

Minor

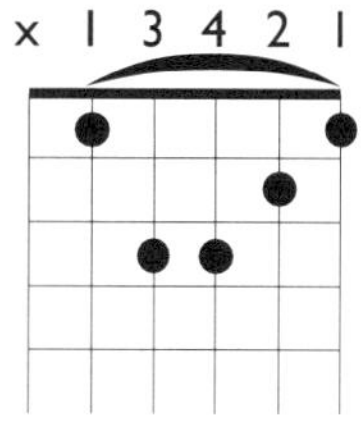

7th

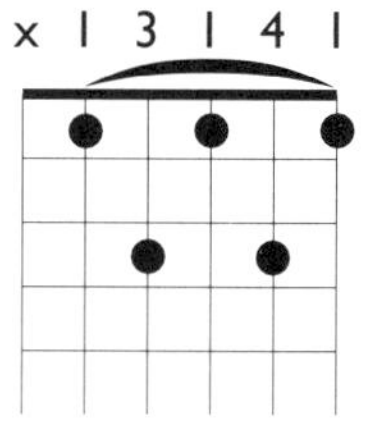

ALTERNATIVE BARRE FINGERINGS

Here are some alternative fingerings that can be useful when you need your 4th finger free to play melodies in a barre chord context: Notice the muted string (x) and the use of the left hand thumb (T).

Major

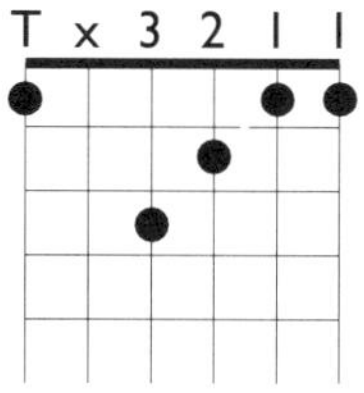

Major

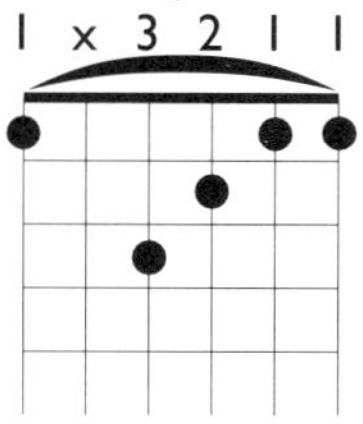

Minor

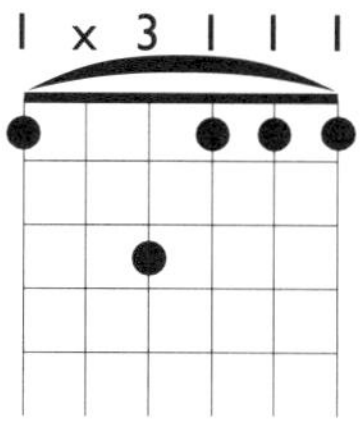

Minor

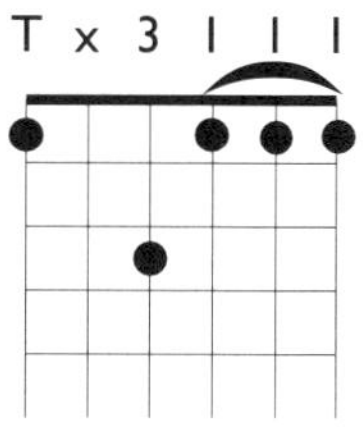

Example 27 will exercise your root 6 chops. These are all root 6 major chords. The pattern begins on the 1st fret (the root is F—the 1st fret of the 6th string) and moves up by a whole step to the 3rd fret (G) and by a whole step again to the 5th fret (A). You might want to study the right hand pattern before practicing the barres.

27

Track 20

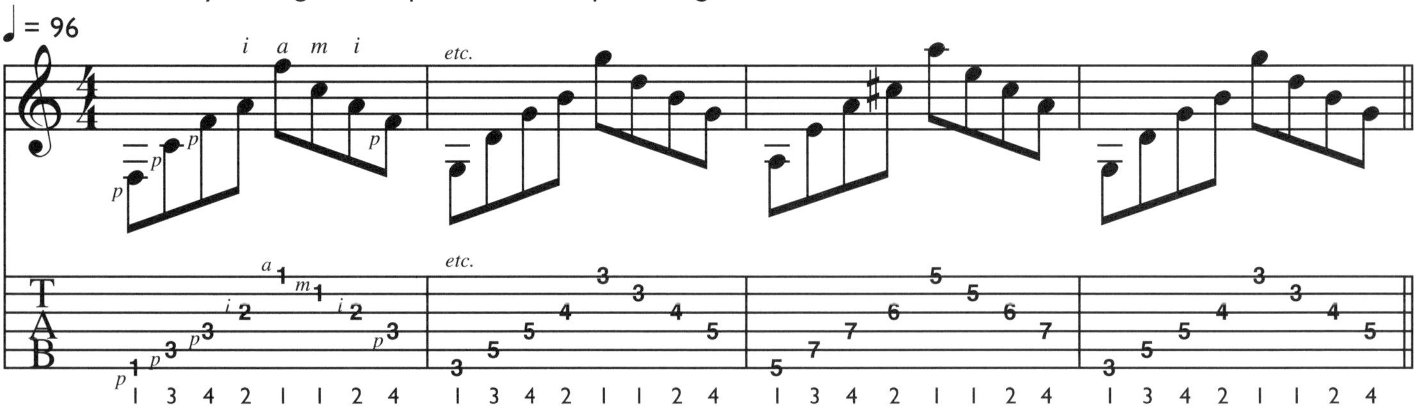

Try the same whole step pattern with other barres and fingerpicking patterns.

28

Track 21

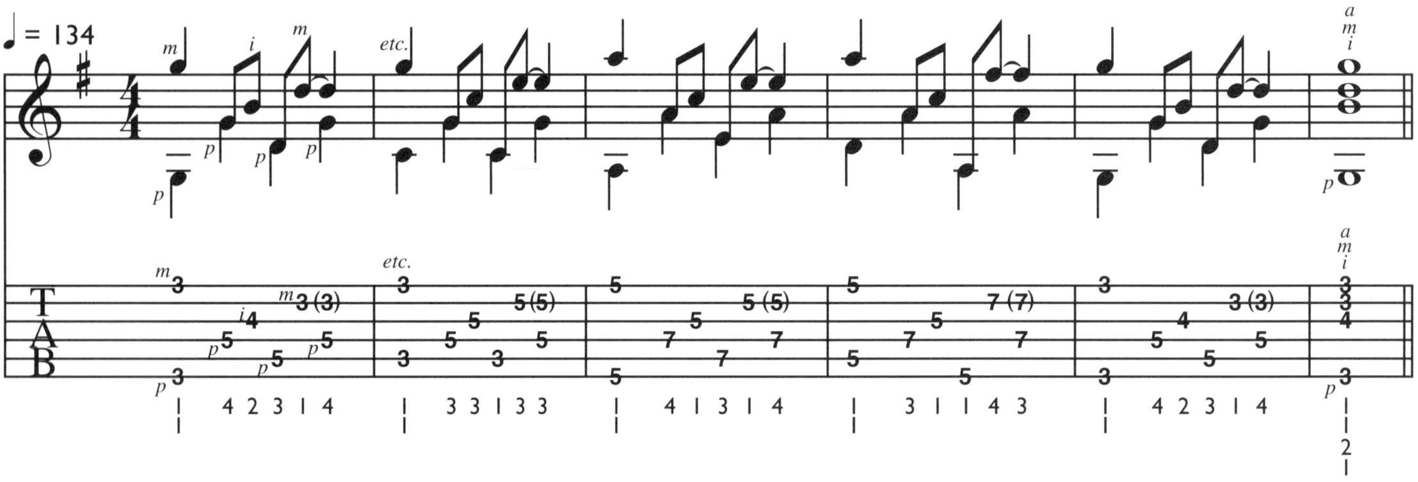

29

Track 22

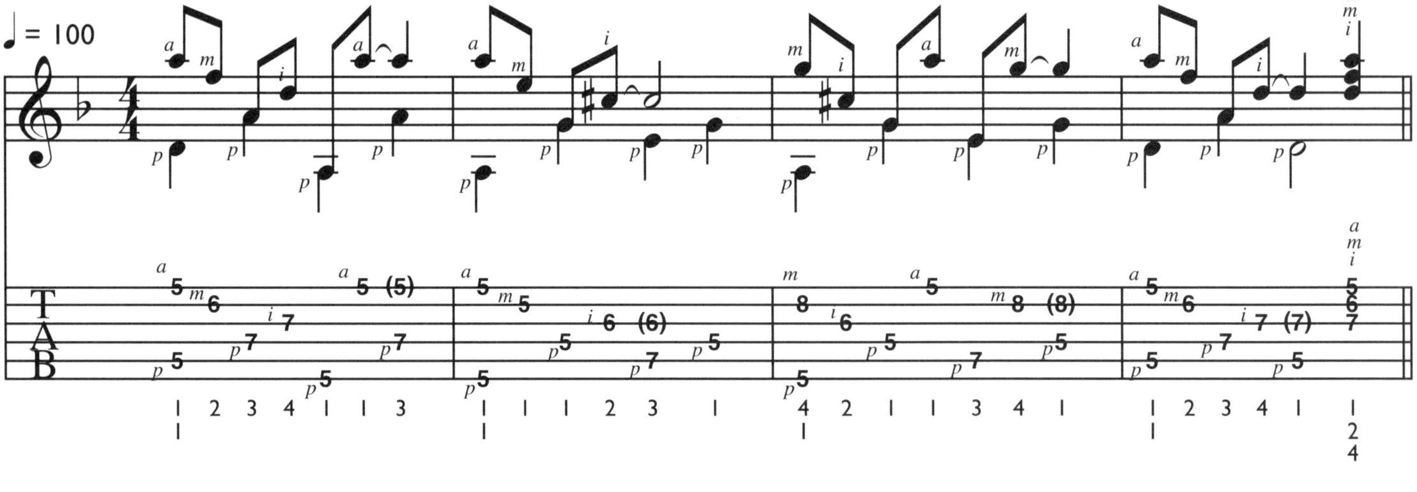

Handle the Barres will flex your root 6 muscles. Be sure to swing the eighths (see page 10).

HANDLE THE BARRES

Track 23

Spanish Nights uses root 5 barres.

SPANISH NIGHTS

Track 24

This piece, in the key of A Minor, relies heavily on minor barre chords.

A MINOR DETAIL

Track 25

CHAPTER 5

More Fingerstyle Patterns

If you are a graduate of *Beginning Fingerstyle Guitar*, and have studied Chapter 2 of this book, you know at least fifteen different fingerstyle patterns, plus, if you've been paying attention, you've noticed numerous other variations in the various pieces in these books. Well, ladies and gentleman, here for your further fingerpickin' enjoyment are four more.

PATTERN #16

This one is really a $\frac{3}{4}$ version of Pattern #10 (see page 13) with quarter notes in the bass.

30

Track 26

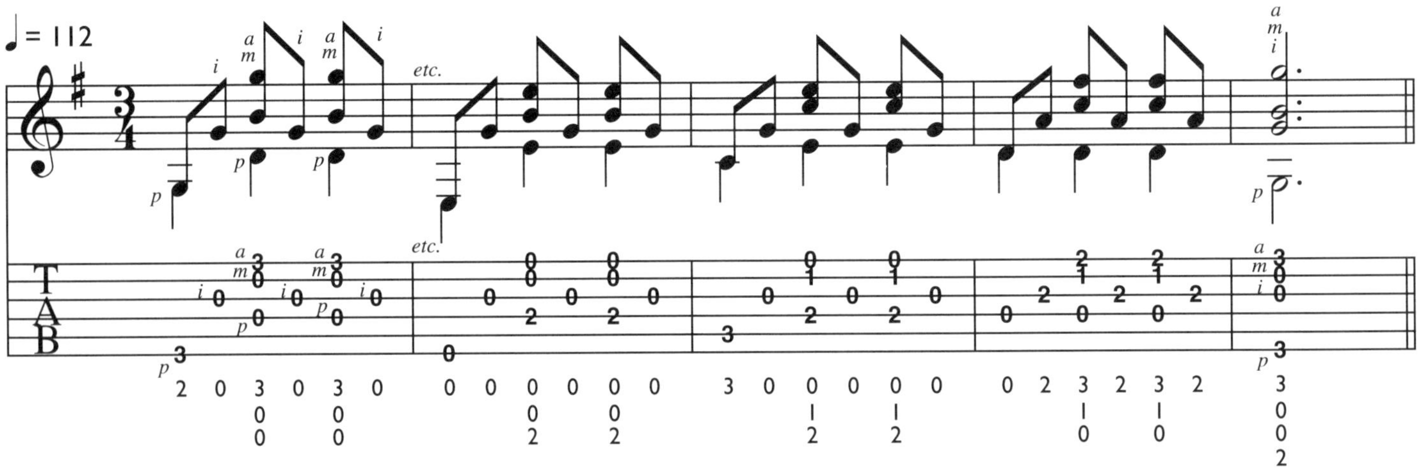

Example 31 will give you some practice with this pattern.

31

Track 27

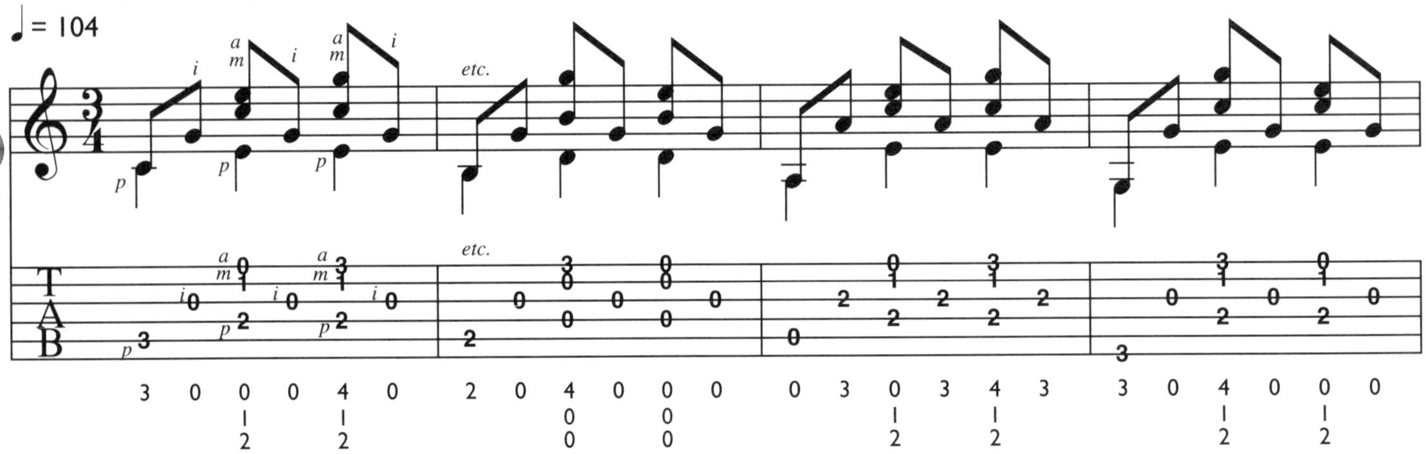

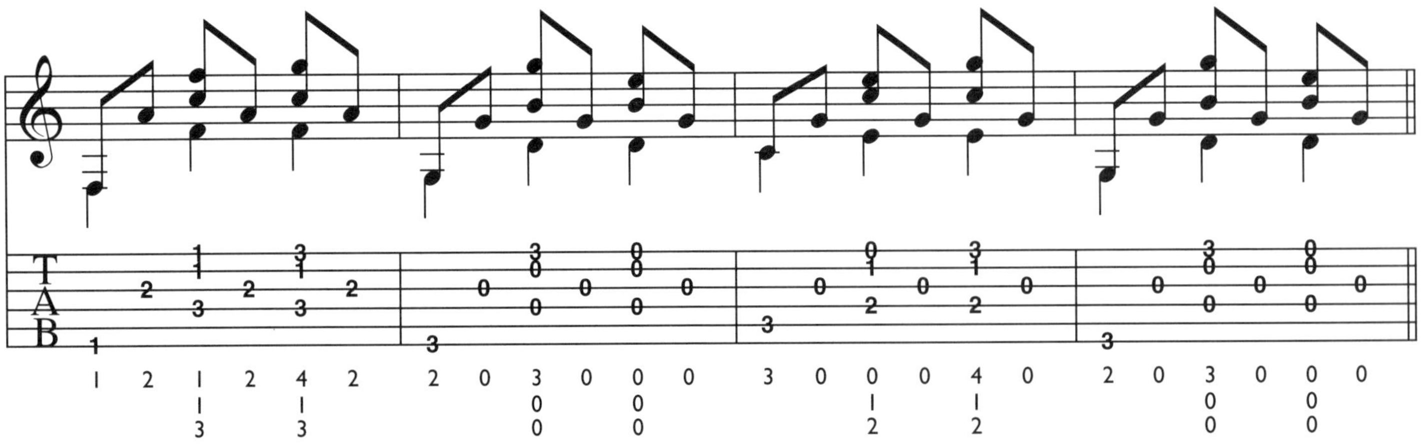

PATTERN #17

Pattern #17 is another alternating bass pattern, much like Pattern #14. There is a nice syncopation in the 3rd beat going into the 4th, spicing up an otherwise straightforward rhythm. Technically, it's easy. Repeating the *m* finger on the first two beats imparts a pleasant, bouncy feel. You may want to watch your right hand at first, to make sure you are crossing from the 1st to 2nd string accurately.

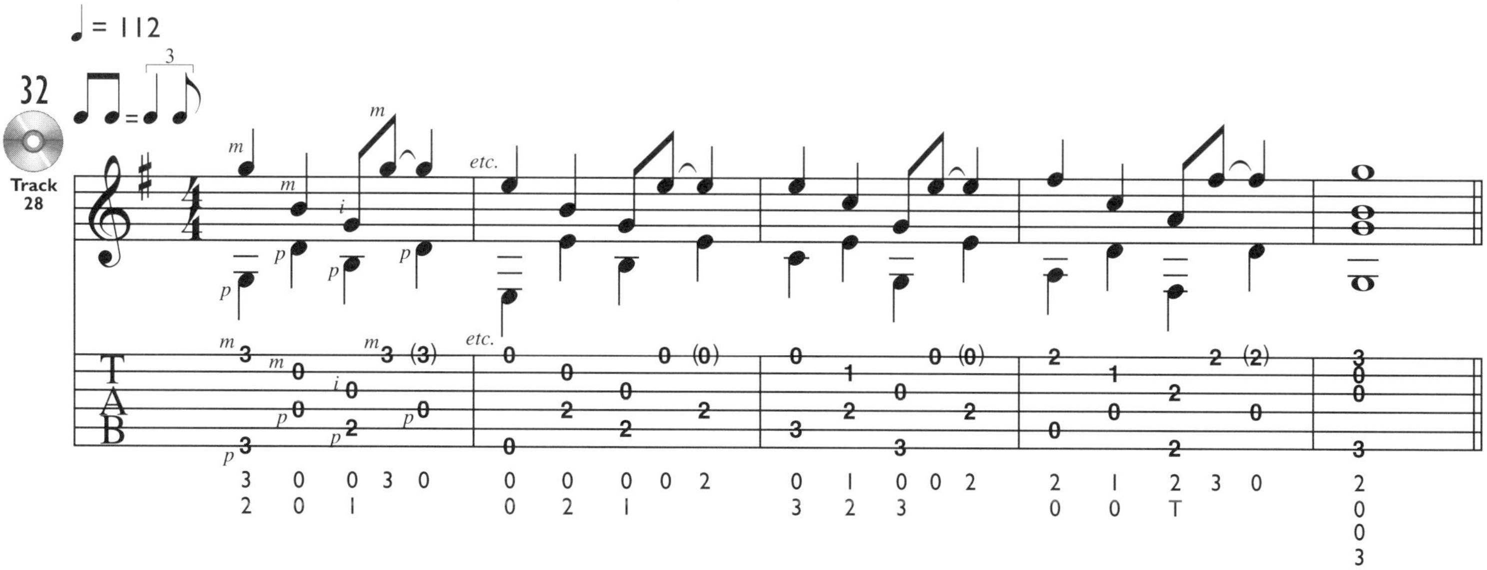

PATTERN #18

Perform the first two beats of Pattern #18 just as you would Pattern #9 (see page 13, or page 55 *Beginning Fingerstyle Guitar*). As you play the *i* stroke on "&" of "2," extend *a*, *m* and *p* to play. After *a* and *p* play, *m* follows into the palm as you re-extend *p* to begin again.

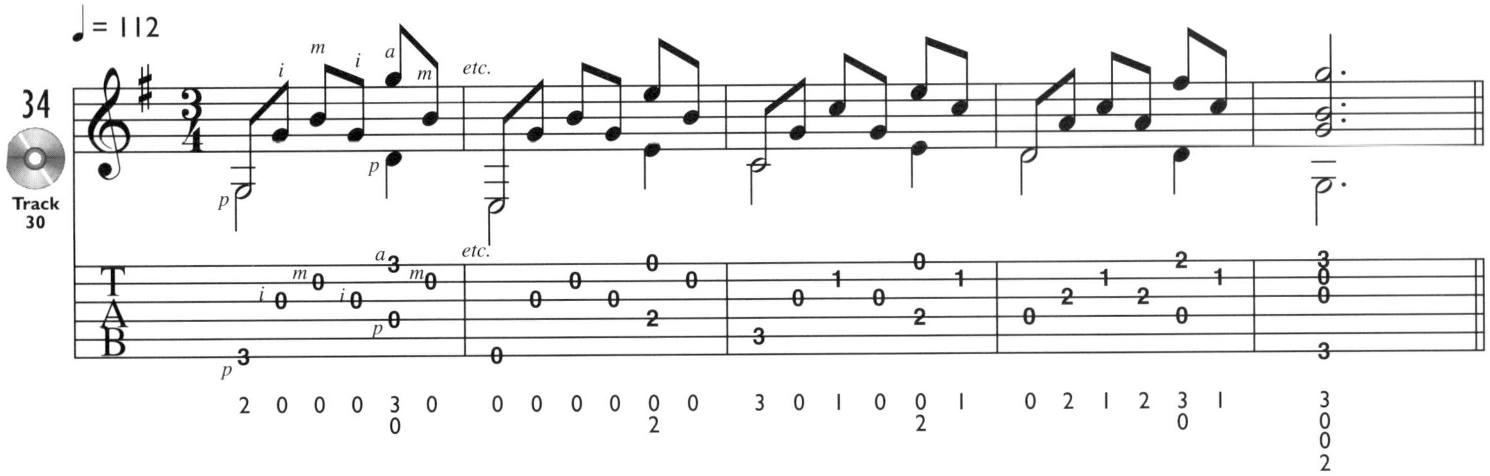

PATTERN #19

Pattern #19 is another variation on the alternating bass, Travis picking pattern. While maintaining the pulsing alternating bass, perform an *i*, *m a* arpeggio as in Pattern #1 (page 12 or *Beginning Fingerstyle Guitar* page 22, but start it off the beat by insterting an *m* stroke on the first half of the first beat and a tie over the third beat.

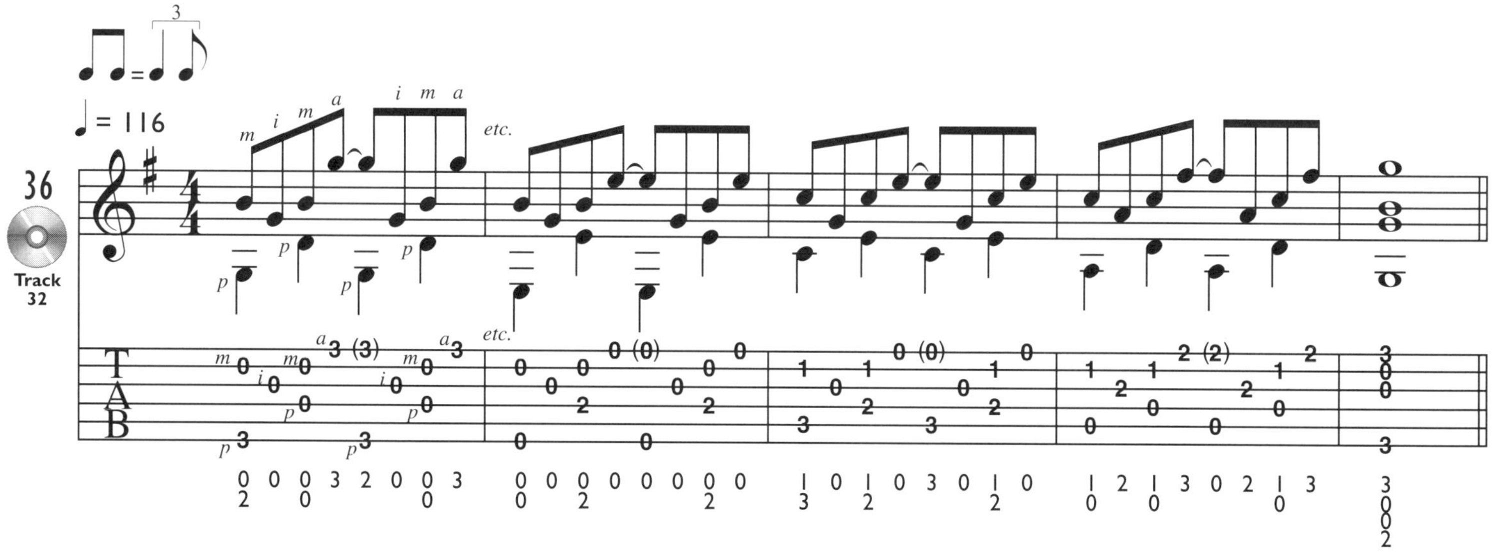

CHAPTER 6

Diatonic Harmony

This chapter will start with a review of what was covered regarding diatonic harmony in *Beginning Fingerstyle Guitar* and then continue into unchartered territory. If you feel you have the major scale and diatonic triads nailed, there's no reason not to turn to the section on 7th chords on page 37.

THE MAJOR SCALE

In order to understand diatonic harmony, you must have a grasp of the major scale. This common scale can begin on any pitch and is made up of a series of whole and half steps. The *formula* of whole steps and half steps is:

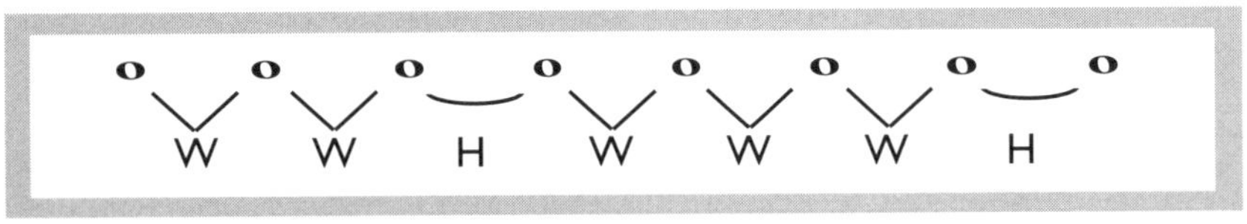

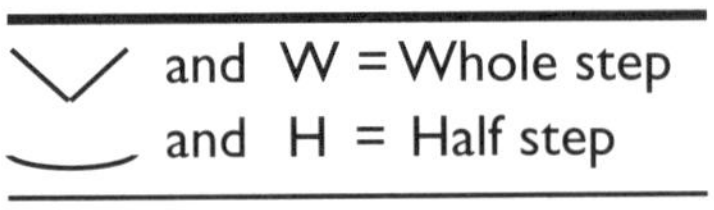

The phrase, "Wendy Witch Has Wild, Wonderful, Wavy Hair" will help you memorize the major scale pattern.

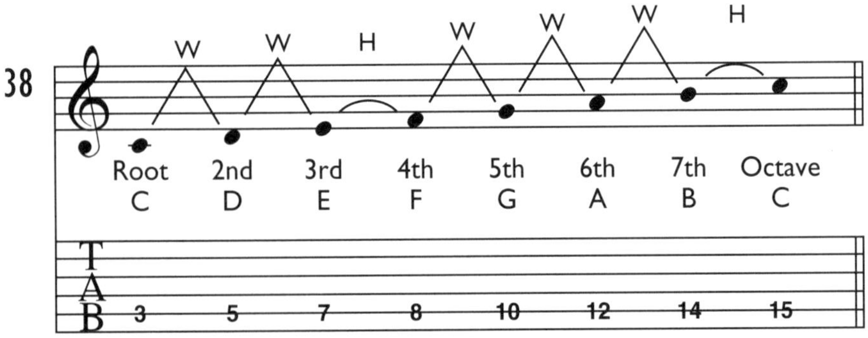

If we build a major scale starting on C, our formula gives us the notes C, D, E, F, G, A, B and C. Playing this scale horizontally up the fifth string, starting with the C on the 3rd fret, enables us to clearly see the pattern of whole and half steps on the neck.

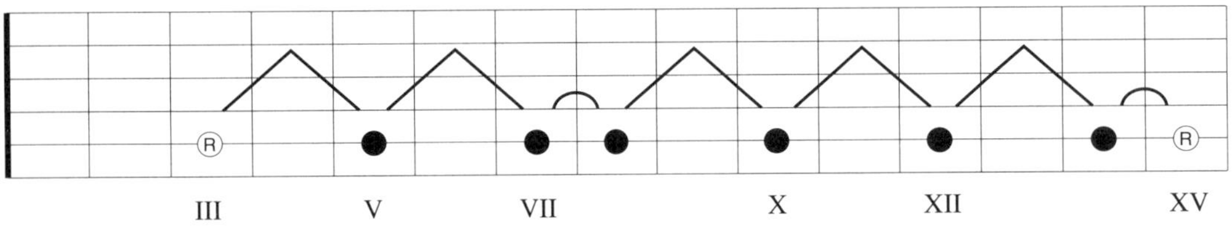

DIATONIC HARMONY—TRIADS

By now, you know the formulas for the most basic chords. Now, we need to see how they are related within one major key. The word *diatonic* means "within the key." For each of the seven different notes in the major scale, we can build a corresponding triad. These are the diatonic triads for that key. There will be a particular pattern of major and minor triads, with a diminished triad at the end, that is the same in any major key.

The following are the diatonic triads in the key of C Major:

39

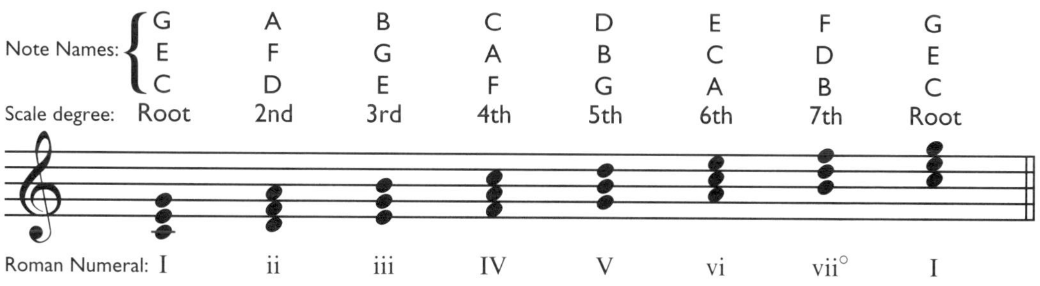

The preferred way to refer to triads is with a number that represents their diatonic position in the key. We use Roman numerals to write these numbers, upper case for major chords (I, IV and V), and lower case for minor (ii, iii and vi). For the diminished triad that occurs on the 7th degree, we add a small circle (○) to a lower-case Roman numeral (vii○). For a quick review of Roman numerals, see page 6.

Here is a summary of the diatonic triads for any major key:

I, IV and V .... are always .... major
ii, iii and vi .... are always .... minor
vii°.................. is always .... diminished

FOUR TYPES OF 7TH CHORDS

Now that you have brushed up on diatonic harmony with triads, it's time to put 7th chords into the mix. First, let's take a look at four important varieties.

THE DOMINANT 7TH CHORD

Frequently, the V chord has another tone added a *minor 3rd* (a distance of three half steps) above the 5th, which is a ♭7 above the root (1 - 3 - 5 - ♭7). This is a called a *dominant 7th* chord. The example on the right shows the V7 chord in the key of C, which is G7.

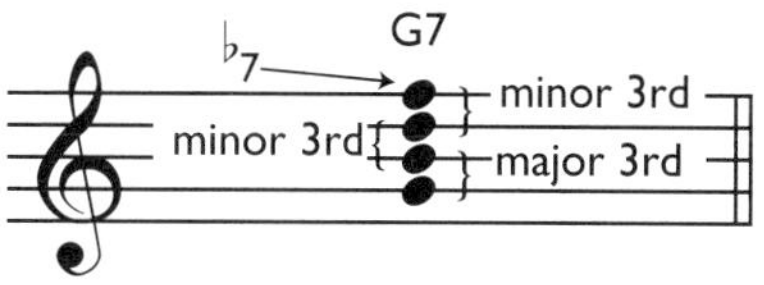

THE MINOR 7TH CHORD

Frequently, the ii, iii or vi chord has another tone added a *minor 3rd* (a distance of three half steps) above the 5th, which is a ♭7 above the root (1 - ♭3 - 5 - ♭7). This is a called a *minor 7th* chord. The example on the right shows the ii7 chord in the key of C, which is Dmin7.

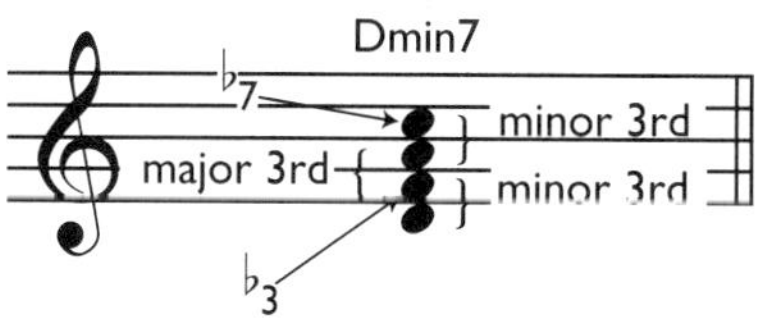

continued on next page...

THE MINOR 7♭5 CHORD

Frequently, the vii○ chord has another tone added a *major 3rd* (a distance of four half steps) above the 5th, which is a ♭7 above the root (1 - ♭3 - ♭5 - ♭7). This is a called a *minor 7♭5* chord. The example on the right shows the min7♭5 chord in the key of C, which is Bmin7♭5. Notice that you can also think of this as a minor 7th chord with a lowered 5 (♭5).

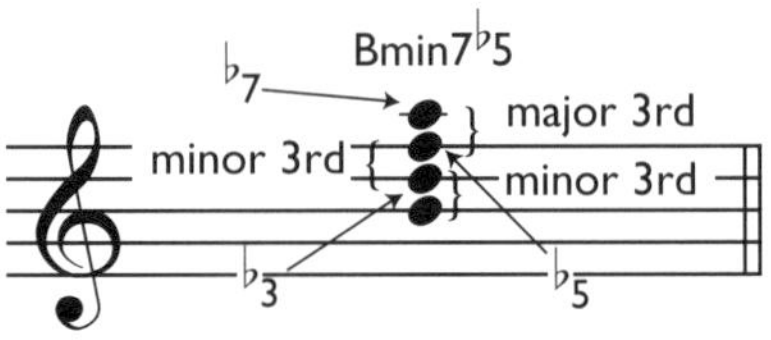

THE MAJOR 7 CHORD

Frequently, the I and the IV chords have another tone added a *major 3rd* (a distance of four half steps) above the 5th, which is a major 7 above the root (1 - 3 - 5 - 7). This is called a *major* 7 chord. The example on the right shows the IV7 chord in the key of C, which is FMaj7.

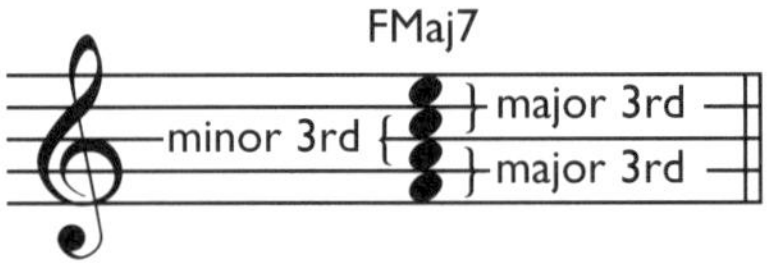

Here are some sample fingerings for the four types of 7th chords you have learned.

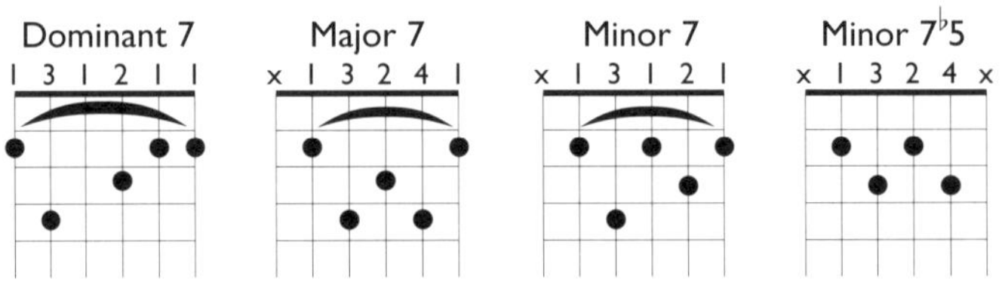

DIATONIC HARMONY—7TH CHORDS

Let's look at the diatonic 7th chords of C Major. Above the triads we generated on page 37, we add another diatonic 3rd. Here's what happens:

40

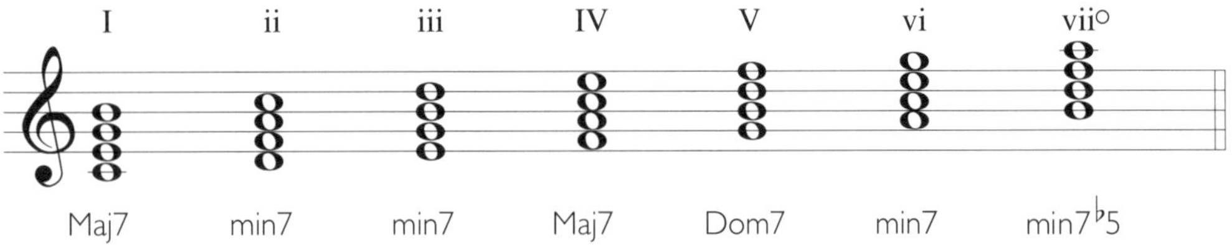

As with the diatonic triads, the diatonic 7th chords have a set pattern of qualities that holds true for every major key. Each triad quality is transformed into a specific quality of 7th chord:

The major triads on I and IV become Maj7 chords. The major triad on V becomes a dominant 7 chord. The minor triads on ii, iii and vi become min7 chords. The diminished triad on vii becomes a min7♭5 chord.

I and IV .... are always .... major 7
V .... is always .... dominant 7
ii, iii and vi .... are always .... minor 7
vii°.................. is always .... minor 7♭5

The following three pieces will get you acquainted with the sounds and applications of the 7th chords. Enjoy.

SEVENTH HEAVEN

Track 34

PHOTO BY LYNN McAFEE/COURTESY OF HASSELBERGER ASSOCIATES

Adrian Legg *is not only a prominent fingerstyle guitarist, but an extraordinary storyteller and a fine photographer. Known for his remarkable technique and eclectic compositional style, he is one of today's most popular players. Check him out in the* Fingerstyle Summit with Adrian Legg, Martin Simpson and Ed Gerhard, *a video produced by the National Guitar Workshop and Alfred.*

HORIZONTAL HOLD

Track 35

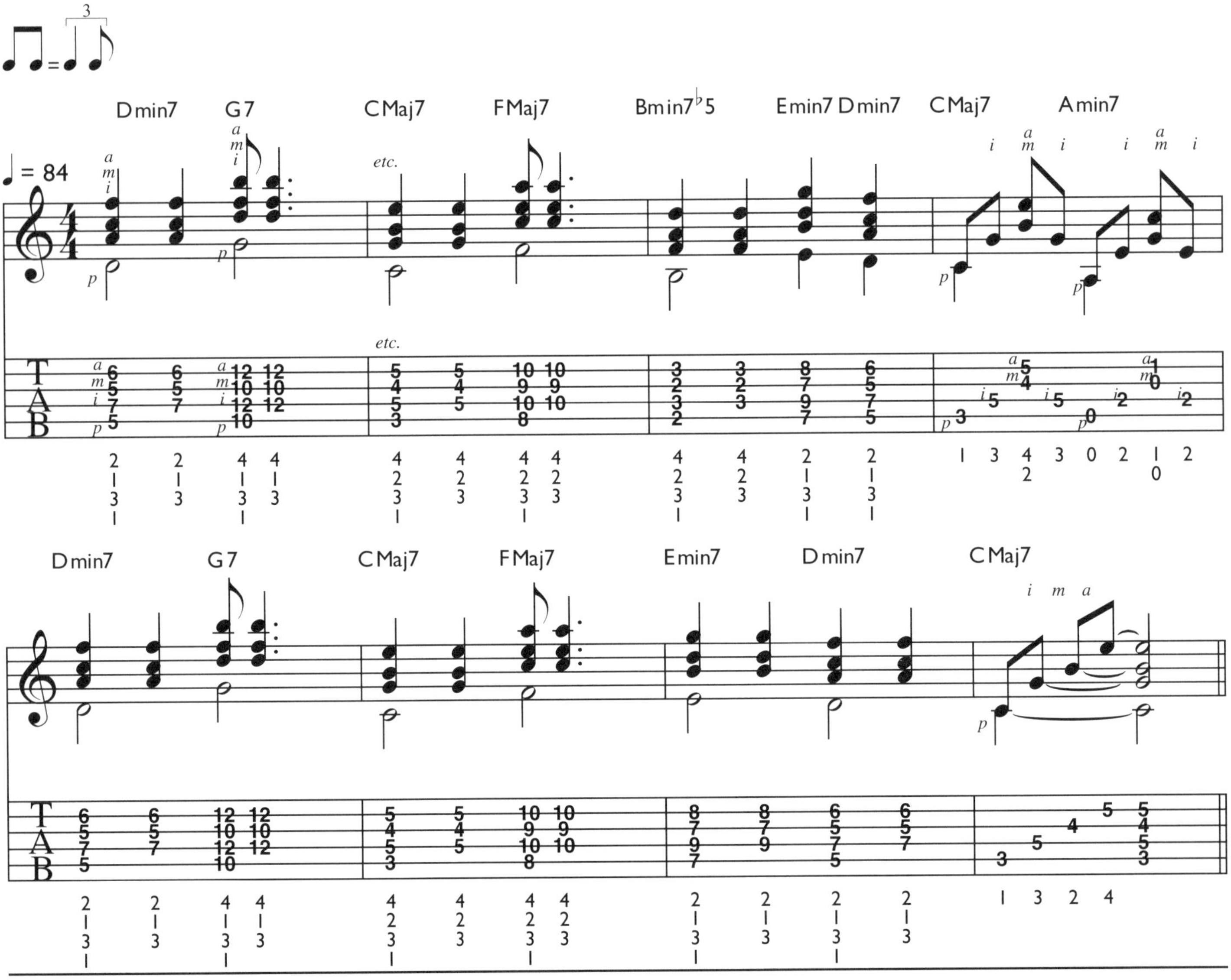

JAZZBERRY JAM

Track 36

PHOTO BY DANA WHEELOCK/COURTESY OF MORRIS, BLIESENER ASSOCIATES

***Leo Kottke** began his career on the leading edge of the fingerstyle guitar movement in the 1960s and '70s. His work—along with the work of a few others, such as John Fahey—inspired a whole new generation of fingerstyle players. Still active as a performer and recording artist, Leo Kottke's playing continues to inspire and instruct.*

CHAPTER 7

Alternate Tunings

One of the most exciting and colorful things about fingerstyle guitar is the wealth of nonstandard or "open" tunings available to players. Many leading artists work with these alternative tunings exclusively, but even those who play mainly in standard tuning will have a few alternate tuning pieces in their repertory. You'll hear alternate tunings in the work of Adrian Legg, Leo Kottke, Michael Hedges, Joni Mitchell, Martin Simpson and almost any other major player.

Beginning Fingerstyle Guitar introduced you to two of the most common alternate tunings, Drop D and Open G. This chapter will review Drop D and Open G and introduce three more important tunings; Open D, DADGAD and Open C. To learn more about this fascinating area check out *Alternate Tunings* by Mark Dziuba, also published by Alfred and the National Guitar Workshop.

DROP D TUNING REVIEW

In drop D tuning we lower the 6th string (E) down a whole step to D. You can do this by using an electric tuner or by using either of the following two methods:

1) Play a harmonic at the 12th fret of the 6th string and tune the 6th string down to match the open 4th string.
2) Play the 7th fret of the 6th string and tune the 6th string down to match the open A 5th string.

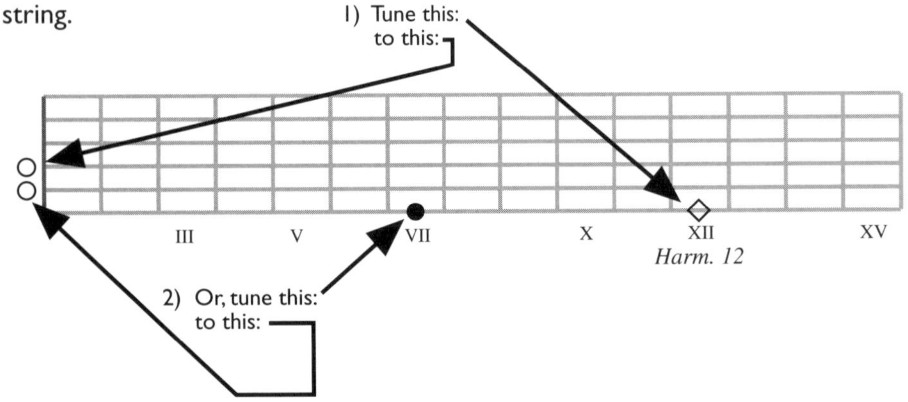

On the next page you will find a Drop D tune in the style of James Taylor. Notice how the hammer-ons, double-stops and syncopations combine to create this style.

NOTES TO JAMES

Track 37

OPEN G TUNING REVIEW

In open G, the strings are tuned D, G, D, G, B, D, from the 6th string to the 1st. The 2nd, 3rd and 4th strings do not change, but the others are lowered to their new pitches. Since a G Major chord is made up of the notes G, B and D, this tuning gives us the sound of a G chord by simply strumming the open strings.

Open G Tuning
Track 38

To tune to G from standard tuning, use an electric tuner or follow these steps:

1. Tune the 6th string down one whole step from low E to Low D. Match the harmonic at the 12th fret of the 6th string to the open 4th string.
2. Tune the 5th string down one whole step from A to G. Match the harmonic at the 12th fret of the of the 5th string to the open 3rd string.
3. Tune the 1st string down one whole step from E to D. Match the open 1st string to the 3rd fret of the 2nd string.

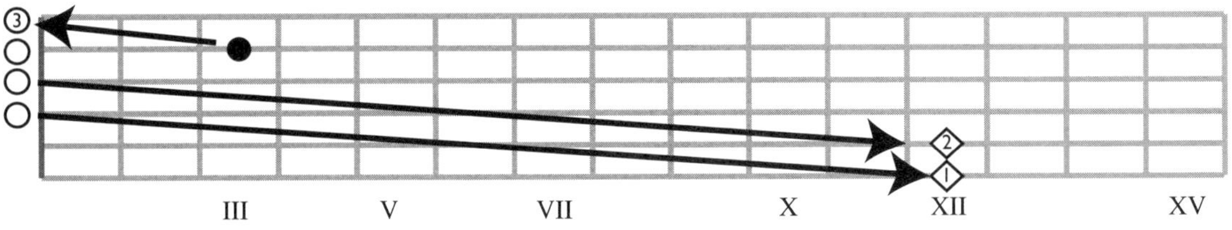

Here's a tune to play in Open G tuning. Be sure to notice the fingerstyle pattern, which is like a detail from the very beginning of Pattern #7 (see page 13 or page 45 of *Beginning Fingerstyle Guitar*). The pattern is *p-m-i-p-a-m* unless otherwise indicated.

ORPHEUS RETURNS

Track 39

D.C. al Coda
Coda

OPEN D TUNING

Open D tuning is very much like open G in that the open strings combine to create a major chord, in this case, D Major. The tuning of the strings, from 6th to 1st, is as follows: D-A-D-F♯-A-D.

Open D Tuning
Track 40

To tune to D from standard tuning, tune to track 40 on the CD, use an electric tuner or follow these steps:

1. Tune the 6th string down one whole step from low E to low D. Match the harmonic at the 12th fret of the 6th string to the open 4th string.
2. Tune the 3rd string down one half step from G to F♯. Match the open 3rd string to the 4th fret of the 4th string.
3. Tune the 2nd string down one whole step from B to A. Match the open 2nd string to the harmonic at the 12th fret of the 5th string.
4. Tune the 1st string down one whole step from E to D. Match the open 1st string to the harmonic at the 12th fret of the 4th string.

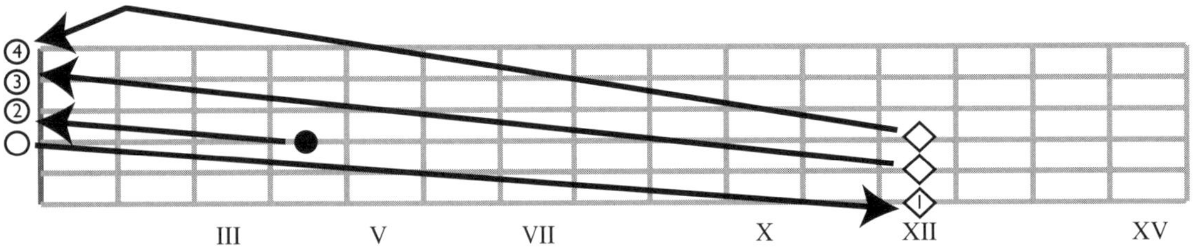

Here are a few chord shapes that will help you get started playing in this tuning:

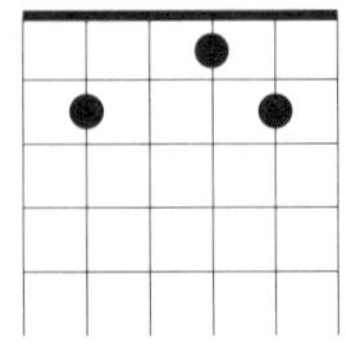

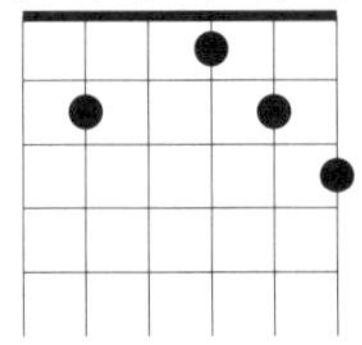

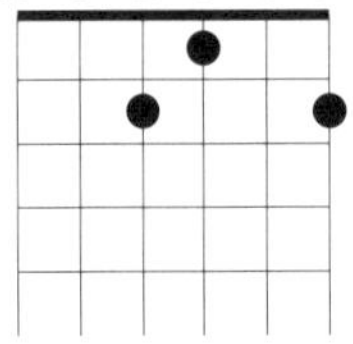

BENDING

Open D lends itself well to the blues style. Accordingly, the next piece, *Blues for Taj*, is in the blues style. It just wouldn't be the blues without a *bend* or two. A bend is accomplished by placing a finger firmly on the string, often with the support of one or two other fingers, and pushing the string up toward the ceiling (1st, 2nd and sometimes 3rd strings) or down toward the floor (6th, 5th, 4th and sometimes 3rd strings). This causes the string's pitch to smoothly move up to the desired pitch. It is an unmistakably bluesy sound that has also become an important tool for rock guitarists. And yes, even we fingerstyle folks have been known to bend a few strings. Check out the work of Adrian Legg. He is one of the world's premier string benders.

In *Blues for Taj* there are two bends. The first, on the very first note of the piece, is a bend on the F on the 8th fret of the 2nd string. This is a half step bend, meaning you only need to bend the string up enough to push the F up to an F♯. Play the F♯ (9th fret, 2nd string) first to learn the sound of the note, and then bend the F up to match that pitch. At the end of the 2nd measure there is a quick bend and release from the F up to F♯ and back to F♮. Simply bend up to F♯ as before, and then quickly release the string back to it's original position. Have fun!

SLIDES

When it comes to playing the blues, *slides* are right up there with bends as an expressive tool. And they're easy. Simply place your left hand finger on the string one or two frets below the destination pitch, such as the F♯ on the first beat of the seventh measure, and slide up to the destination. Keep an even pressure on the string as you slide, so that you hear the sliding sound. Slides are usually performed right on the beat.

BLUES FOR TAJ

Track 51

DADGAD TUNING

DADGAD tuning (said dad-gad) is one of the most important alternate tunings used by fingerstyle guitarists. Some of the guitar's greatest exponents, such as Jimmy Page and John Renbourne, have used this tuning. The brilliant French Algerian guitarist, Pierre Bensusan, uses DADGAD almost exclusively. This tuning has a very unique sound and, when paired with some of the expressive devices introduced in this section, will produce the highly distinctive sound we associate with Bensusan.

Track 42

To tune to DADGAD from standard tuning, use an electric tuner, tune to Track 42 on the CD, or follow these steps:

1. Tune the 6th string down one whole step from low E to low D. Match the harmonic on the 12 fret of the 6th string to the open 4th string.
2. Tune the 2nd string down one whole step from B to A. Match the open 2nd string to the harmonic on the 12th fret of the 5th string.
3. Tune the 1st string one whole step from E to D. Match the open 1st string to the harmonic at the 12th fret of the 4th string.

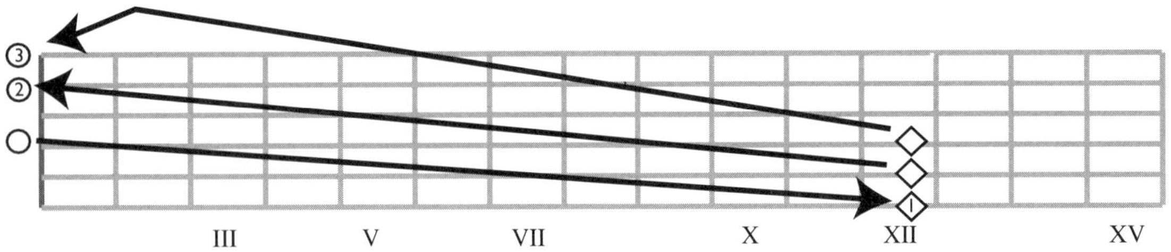

Here are some useful DADGAD chord shapes that you should learn:

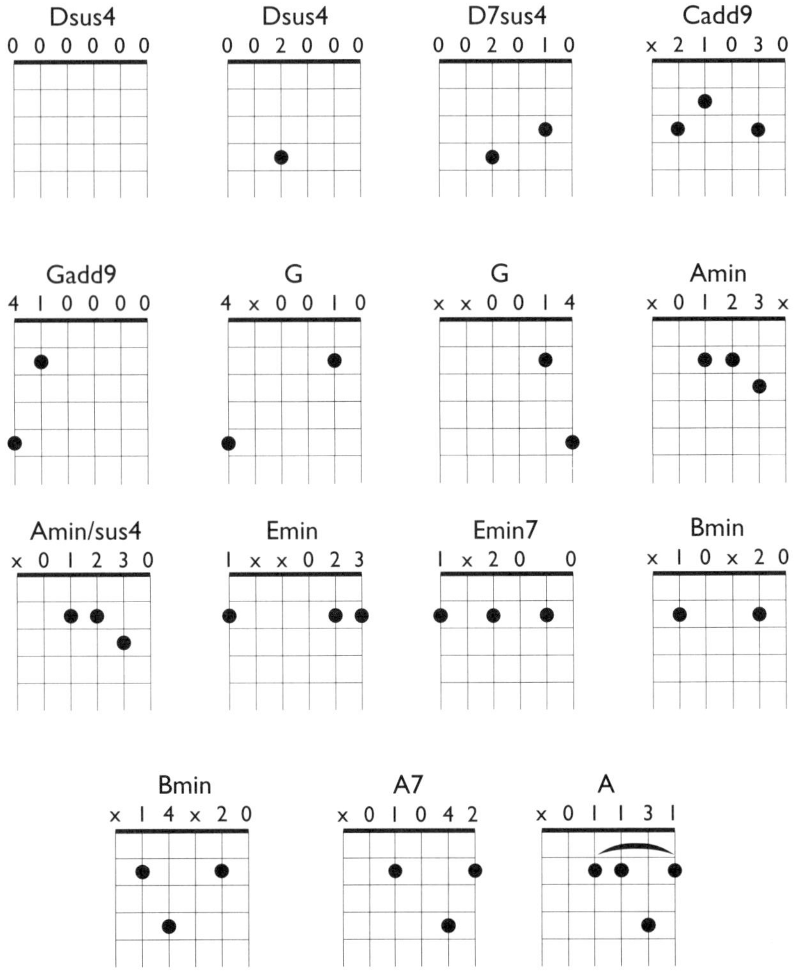

EXPRESSIVE DEVICES THAT SOUND GREAT IN DADGAD

If you want to play in the style of the great Pierre Bensusan, or use his style as an inspiration to find your own voice, you should learn these techniques.

Here are four examples demonstrating how well the *harp technique* you learned on page 70 of *Beginning Fingerstyle Guitar* works in DADGAD. The notes of a scale are played across different strings, allowing them to ring through one another.

41

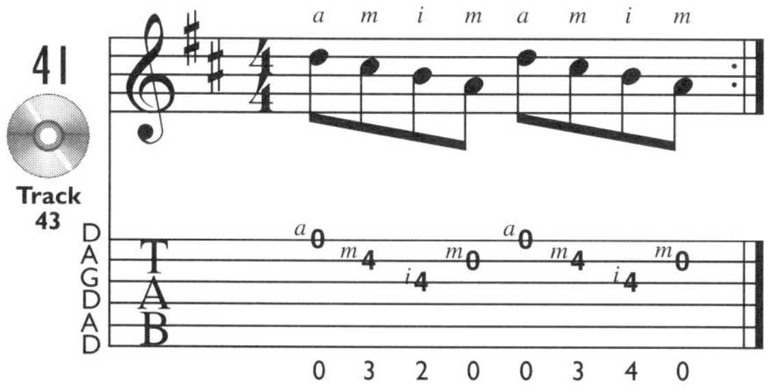

42

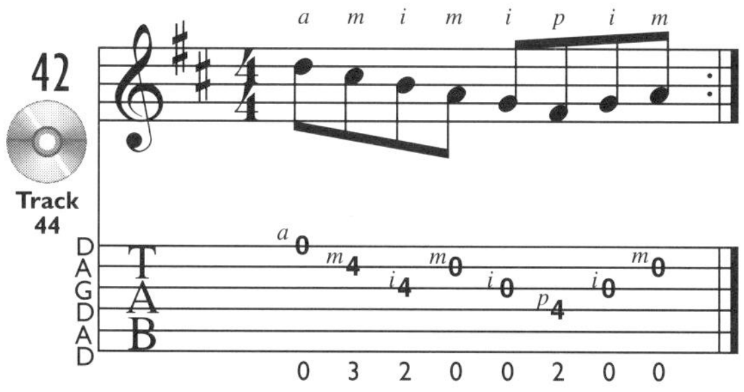

43

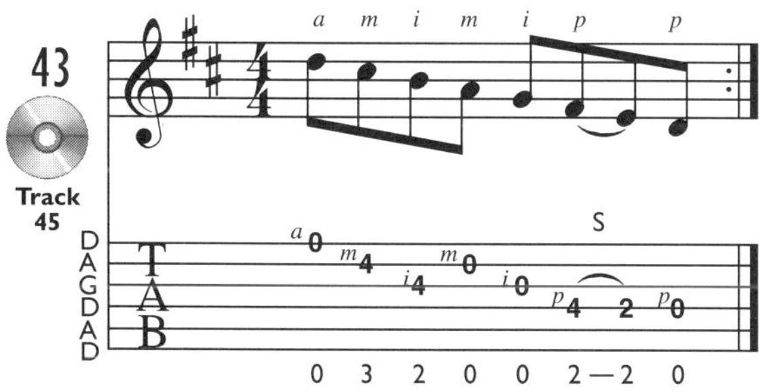

44

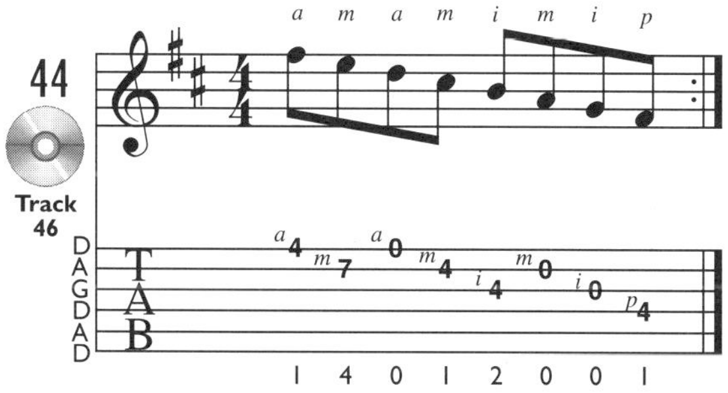

Example 45 involves *palm muting*. Place the pinky side of your right hand palm on the bass strings (6th, 5th and 4th) just next to the bridge. Strike the bass strings with *p*. This will produce a slightly muffled but still pitched sound.

This is a great technique. Sometimes called a *"Bartok Pizz.,"* sometimes called a *"pop,"* this percussive effect is made by pulling the string out slightly from the guitar with the right hand and letting it go, causing it to slap against the frets.

45

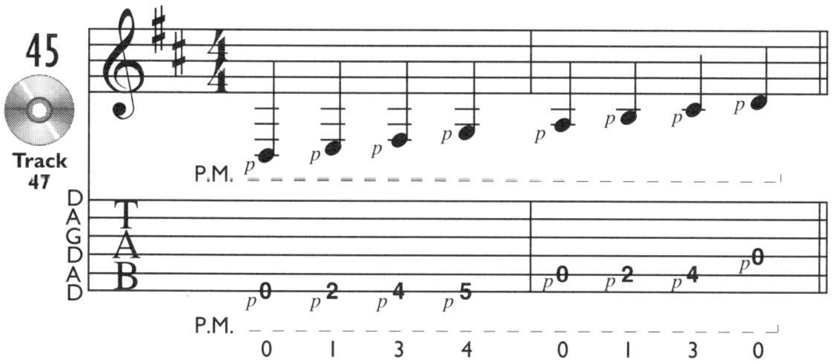

46

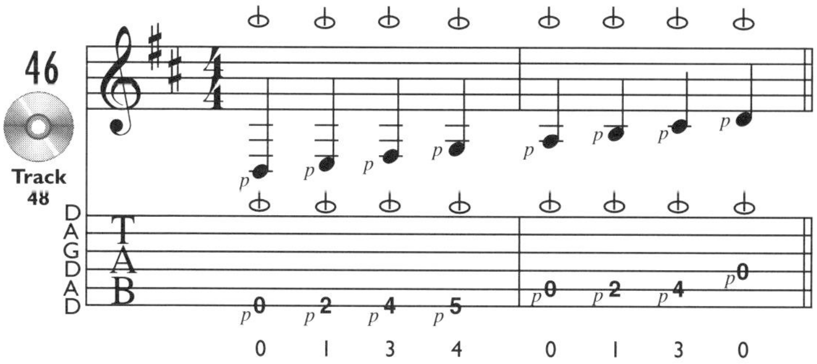

Try mixing palm muting and popping. Use the *p* finger to do both.

P.M. = palm mute
⦶ = pop or Bartok Pizz.

47

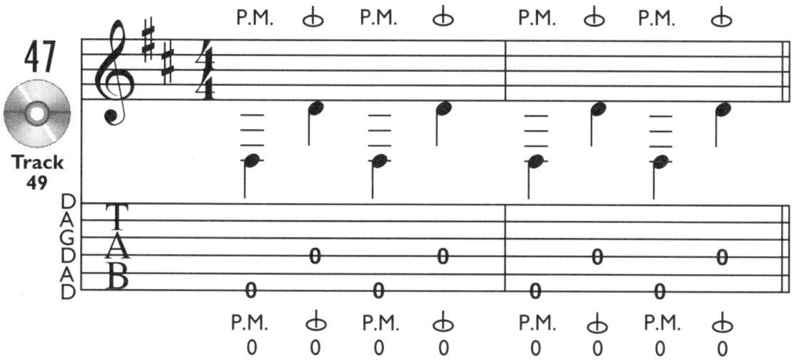

Now try adding a melody to the groove you created in Example 47. Use *m* and *i* on the melody and *p* on your palm mute and pop bass figure. Just be careful to mute only the bass strings so that the melody will sing clearly.

48

Track 50

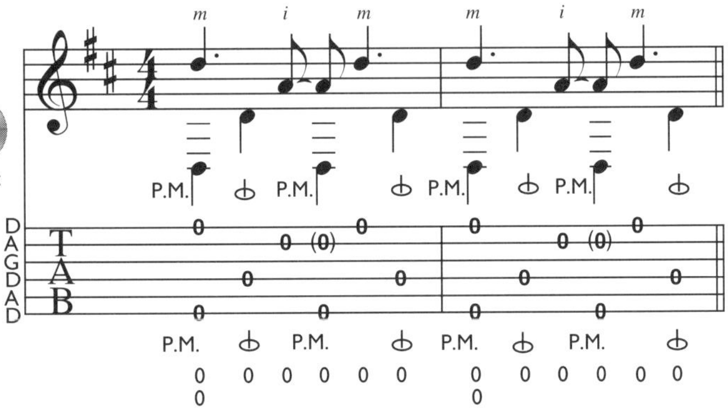

Example 49 includes palm muted notes that are also popped. For extra expressivity, a wide, intense *vibrato* 〰 is added to the syncopated C♯. The vibrato is performed by rapidly pushing the string up and down a small distance, causing a very small pitch waver, similar to a vocal vibrato.

49

Track 51

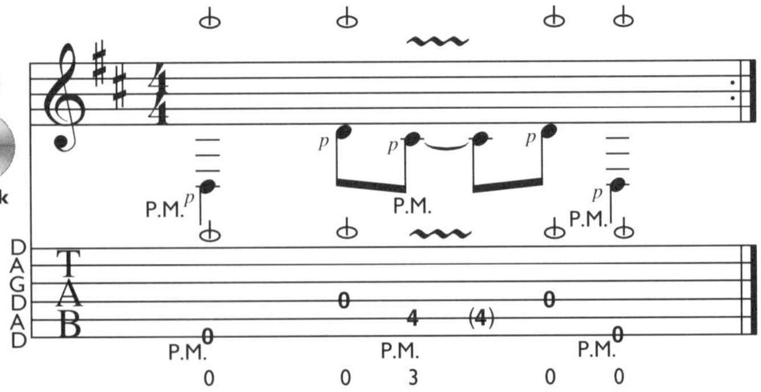

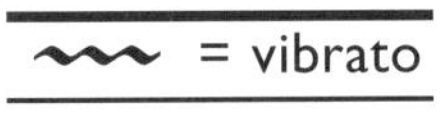

This example puts all these new techniques together: harp technique, palm muting, popping and vibrato. Then, dig into *For Pierre* on the next page and have fun!

50

Track 52

FOR PIERRE

Track 53

OPEN C TUNING

This is another great example of an open tuning. When the open strings are strummed, they sound a C Major chord. In open C, the strings are tuned C-G-C-G-C-E from 6th to 1st.

Track 54

To tune to open C from standard tuning, use an electric tuner, tune to Track 54 on the CD, or follow these steps:

1. Tune the 6th string down two whole steps from E to C. Match the harmonic at the 12th fret of the 6th string to the 3rd fret of then 5th string.
2. Tune the 5th string down one whole step from A to G. Match the harmonic at the 12th fret of the 5th string to the open 3rd string.
3. Tune the 4th string down one whole step from D to C. Match the open 4th string to the harmonic at the 12th fret of the altered 6th string.
4. Tune the 2nd string up one half step from B to C. Match the 2nd string open to the harmonic at the 12th fret of the altered 4th string.

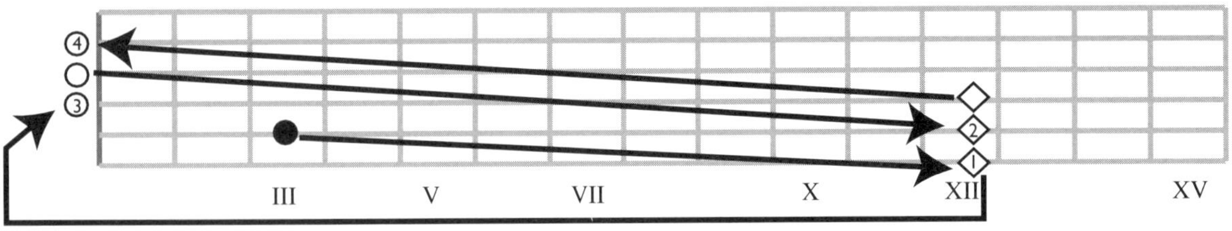

PHOTO COURTESY OF KAMAN MUSIC

***Badi Assad** is one of the most unique and gifted artists to appear on the scene in the 1990s. She combines classical technique, Latin rhythms and unusual vocal techniques to create a completely original style of music.*

SEEING YOU AGAIN

Track 55

CHAPTER 8

Inversions

INVERTING THE TRIADS

Every triad can be inverted. An inverted triad is one whose bass (lowest note) is one other than the root. Because there are three notes in a triad there are only three basic ways to voice (arrange) a triad.

A root position triad has its root in the bass.
A 1st inversion triad has its 3rd in the bass.
A 2nd inversion triad has its 5th in the bass.

For instance, a root position C Major triad has C as the bass. In 1st inversion, E is the bass, and in 2nd inversion G is the bass. The arrangement of the notes above the bass (voicing) is up to you. If all three chord tones appear at least once, the chord is correct.

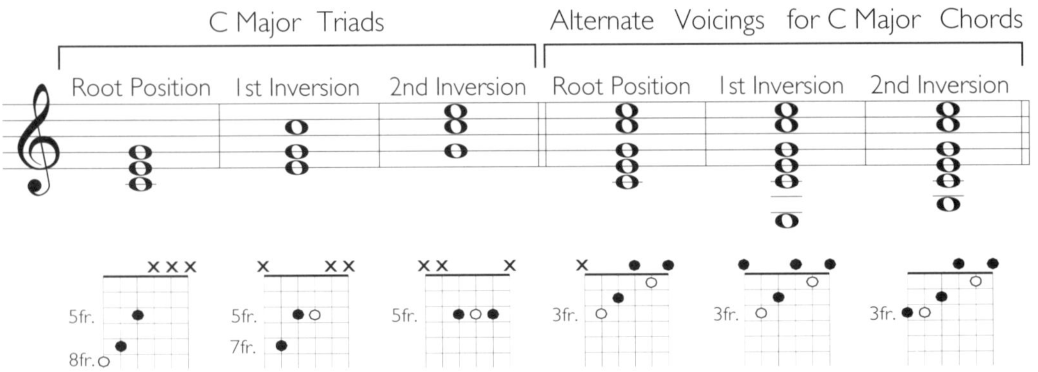

O = Root

SLASH CHORD NOTATION

Slash chord notation is a common method for notating inversions. In slash chord notation, the root of the chord is written, followed by a slash and the name of the lowest note of the chord. In slash notation, a 1st inversion C Major triad would be written as **C/E**. C is the root, and E is the bass. A 2nd inversion C Major triad would be written as **C/G.** C is again the root, and G is the bass. The example below shows basic triads, and typical voicings of these chords, as slash chords.

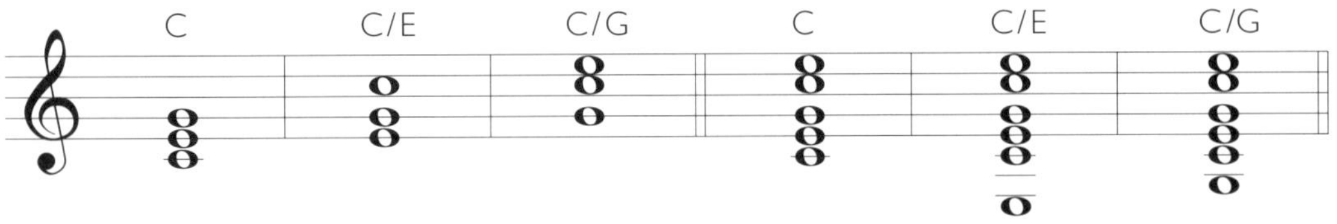

INVERSIONS ON THE TOP THREE STRINGS

The next three exercises will help you get more familiar with inverting triads. Each of the examples harmonizes the diatonic triads in the key of C on the top three strings (1st, 2nd and 3rd) over the first twelve frets. Notice that minor and diminished chords are inverted in exactly the same manner as major chords. Play through each example slowly at first, and pay close attention to the fingerings for each inversion of each chord type. Each example will begin with whatever triad falls in open position.

ROOT POSITION TRIADS IN C MAJOR

51

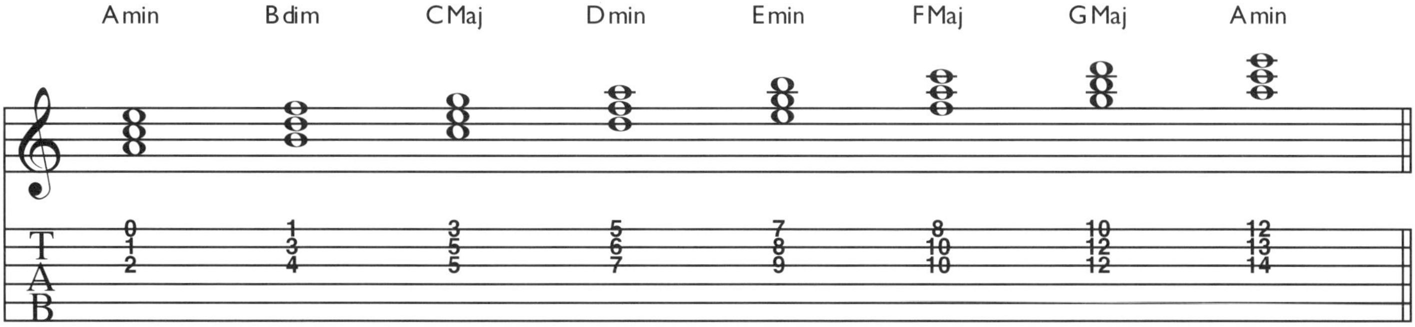

1ST INVERSION TRIADS IN C MAJOR

52

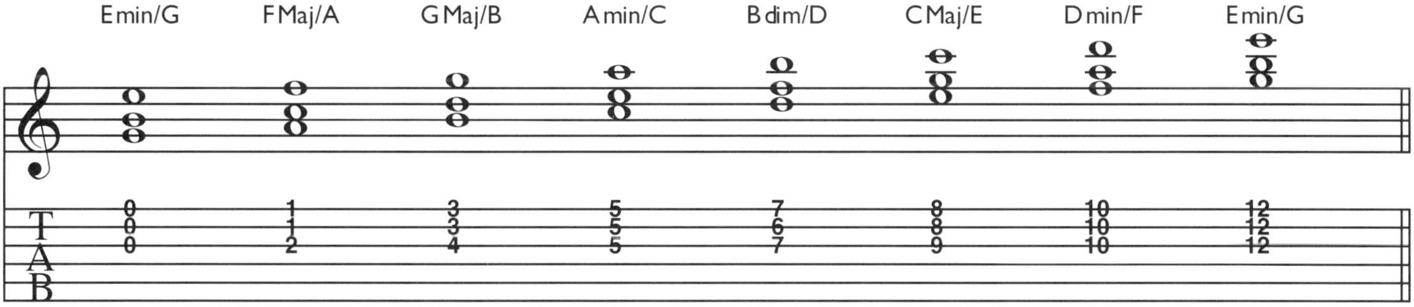

2ND INVERSION TRIADS IN C MAJOR

53

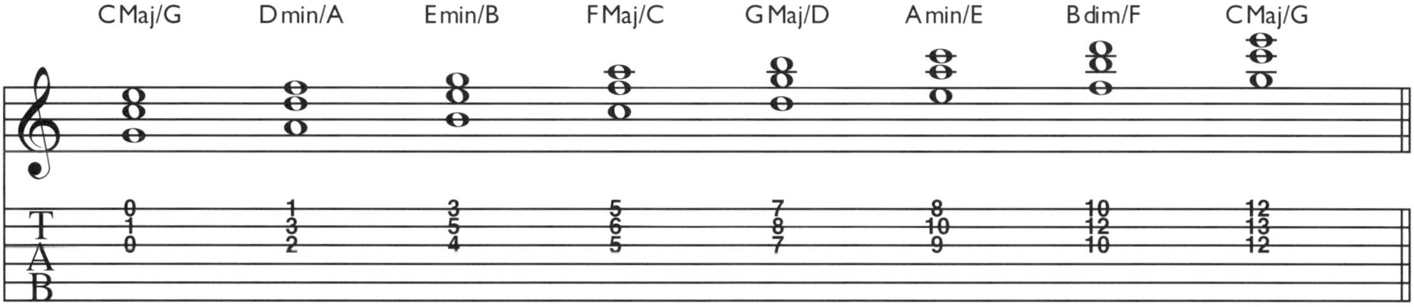

By now, you have played hundreds of inversions, whether you knew it or not! For instance, every time we play an alternating bass, we are playing root position chords alternating with 1st and 2nd inversion chords. Go back and look at some of the fingerstyle patterns and you'll see inversions all over the place. They are an integral part of fingerstyle playing. Now that you have studied them specifically, learn the following selections in which inversions were used to create the pieces. Try to be aware of which inversion you are playing at any given time. Have fun.

Track 56

BUDDY'S BACK

THREE'S IN THREE

Track 57

INVERSIONS ON THE 4TH, 3RD AND 2ND STRINGS

The following examples, in A Major this time, will familiarize you with the inversions on the 4th, 3rd and 2nd strings. Master them before moving on to the next piece. Each example will begin with whatever triad falls in the open position.

ROOT POSITION CHORDS ON THE 4TH, 3RD AND 2ND STRINGS

54
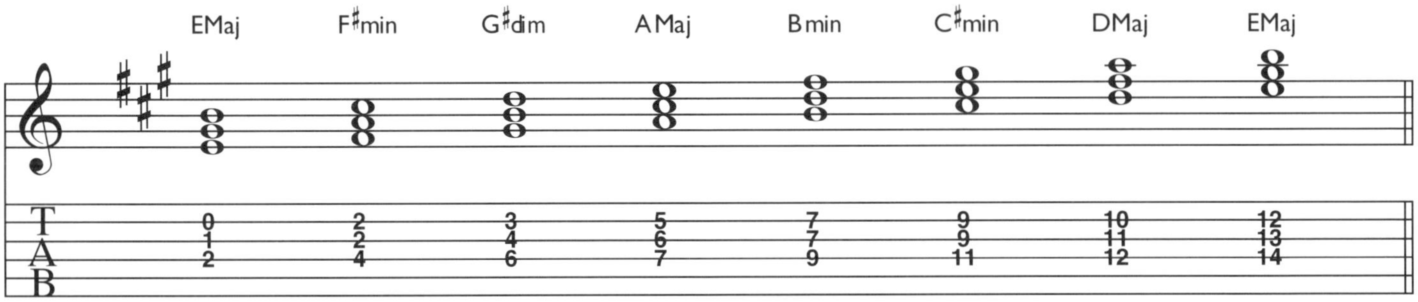

1ST INVERSION CHORDS ON THE 4TH, 3RD AND 2ND STRINGS

55
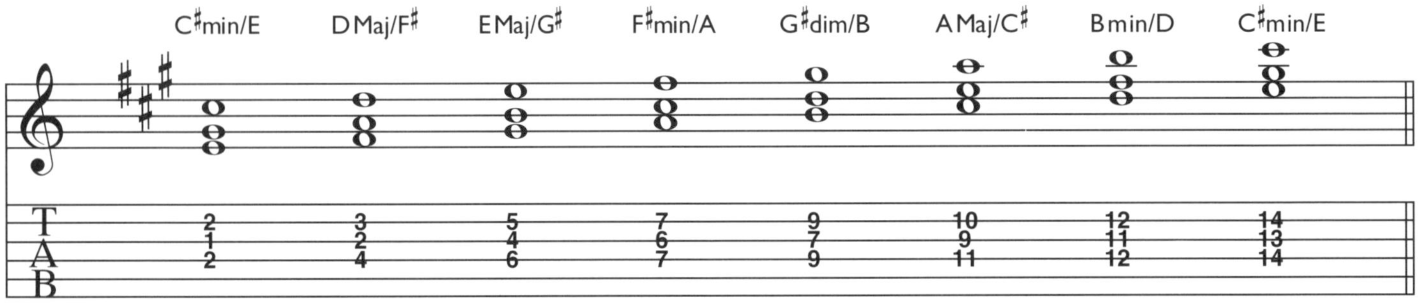

2ND INVERSION CHORDS ON THE 4TH, 3RD AND 2ND STRINGS

56
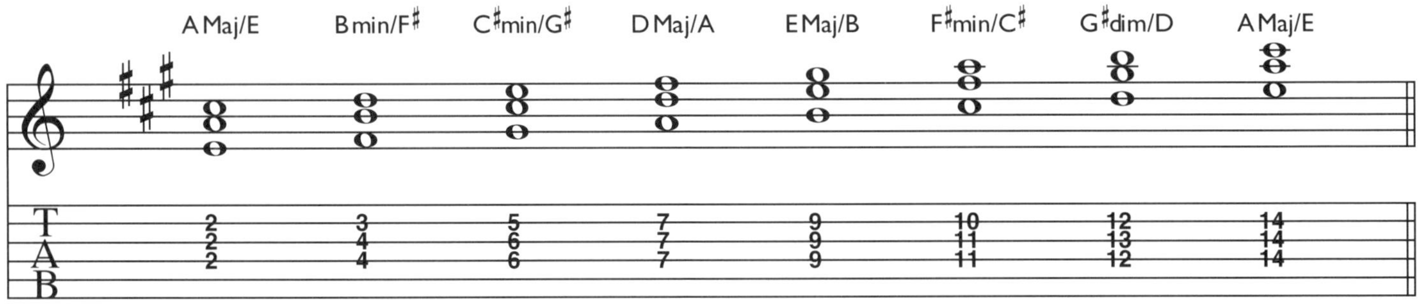

HAMMERING AWAY

Track 58

TER 9

Exploring Bass Lines

One of the coolest things about playing fingerstyle guitar is that we can play all the parts of a piece or arrangement simultaneously—we can play the melody, accompaniment and bass line all at once. Do you remember hearing that piece that got you interested in fingerstyle guitar? *"You mean to tell me that's ONE guitarist?!"*

In large part, that's what it's all about to play fingerstyle. And, to a very significant degree, a strong piece or arrangement is one with a really strong bass line. As fingerstylists, we spend a lot of time—maybe too much time—playing alternating bass lines (as in Travis picking). But to be stuck in that style of playing is very limiting. One of the most important things you can do to expand your horizons as an arranger, composer or player is to break away from the alternating bass and start working with lines. We began exploring this topic in Chapter 10 of *Beginning Fingerstyle Guitar* and will expand on it in this chapter.

WALKING BASS LINES—REVIEW

Walking bass lines are scale passages played by *p* in the lower strings. In some pieces, these bass lines are so distinctive they make the chords, and even the melody, seem secondary. The chord pattern and melody can be created to fit the bass, rather than the other way around. Ideally, the bass fits the melody like a glove.

Study this walking bass line. Then learn *Walking Around* on page 61 and notice how it fits the melody and moves through the different harmonies.

57

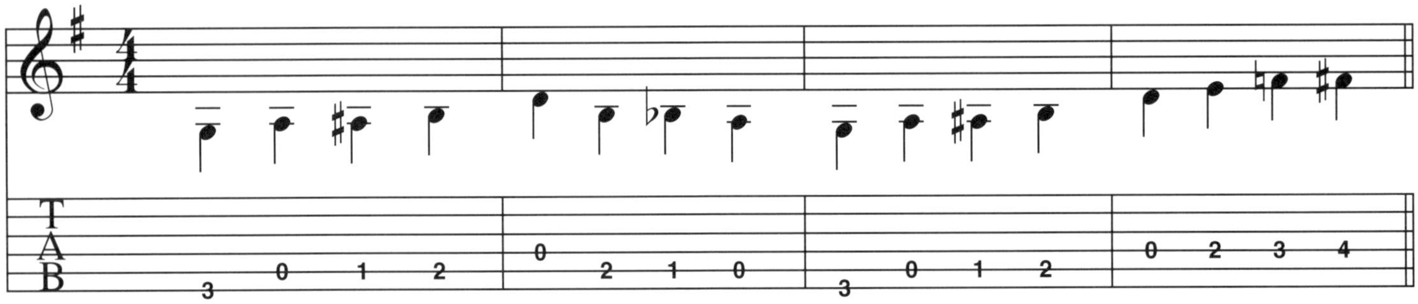

WALKING AROUND

Track 59

GOIN' DOWN

Track 60

BOOGIE BEAT

Track 61

ARPEGGIO BASS LINES

As you learned on page 22 of *Beginning Fingerstyle Guitar*, in an arpeggio the notes of a chord are played individually, rather than all together. Arpeggios are the fingerstyle guitarist's bread and butter. They are useful for accompaniments (virtually all of the fingerstyle patterns you have learned are arpeggios), they can include melody and accompaniment and they make great bass lines.

Here are two arpeggio bass lines that you will probably recognize. The 1950s and '60s may have been cancelled without them. Use your theory knowledge to figure out what they are (turn the book upside down to read the answer at the bottom of this page).

58

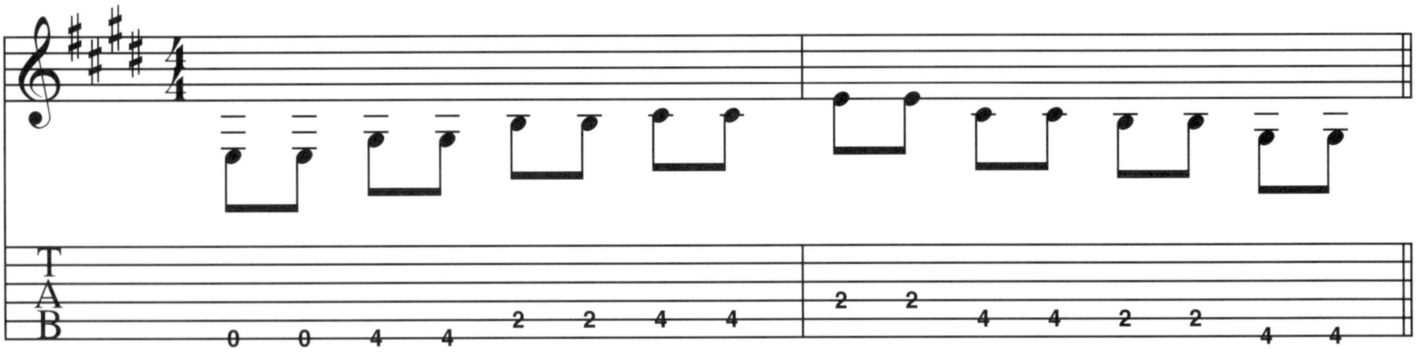

59

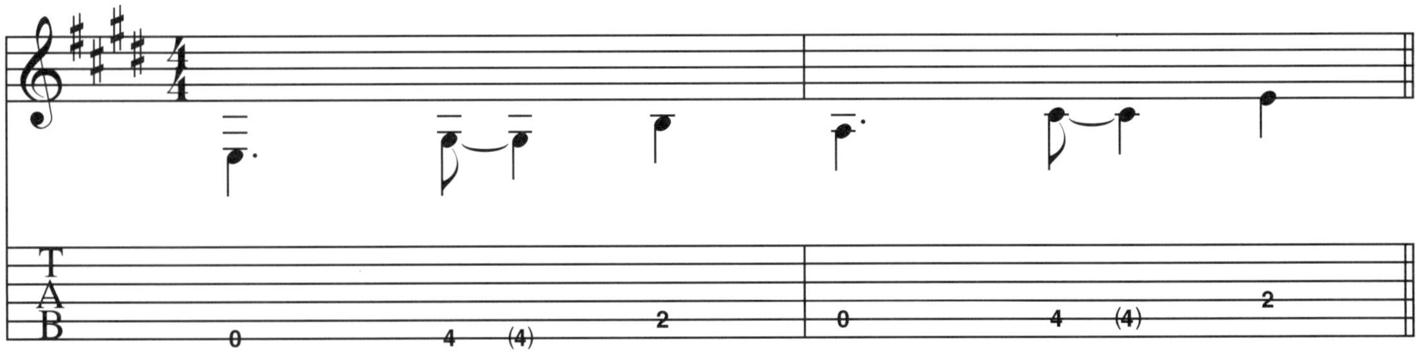

Ray's Rockin' on page 65 is a great example of a piece using an arpeggiated bass line. Learn it well and enjoy!

Answer: E Major and A Major.

RAY'S ROCKIN'

Track
62

CHAPTER 10

The Modes

Every type of scale evokes a certain mood which is related to how the half steps fall in the scale pattern. The familiar major scale (also called the Ionian mode) has a "bright" or "up" feeling. The natural minor scale (Aeolian mode) that we examined in Chapter 5 of *Beginning Fingerstyle Guitar* has a more somber or "dark" quality.

By starting a scale from each note of the major scale, and using the same set of notes belonging to that major scale, we can create all the *modes* of the major scale. In other words, a mode is a re-ordering of the notes of a scale. This approach to viewing the modes is often called the relative approach. You can also view each mode as being parallel to a major scale of the same root. These are exactly the same concepts as the relative and parallel minor that you learned about in Chapter 5 of *Beginning Fingerstyle Guitar*.

Besides the Ionian and Aeolian modes the two modes of the major scale most common to rock music are the *Dorian* and *Mixolydian* modes. These names come from the names of Greek tribes whose music was originally associated with these sounds.

The following example shows the modes of the C Major scale and the chord type most related to each mode. For instance, we think of a minor 7th chord as being closely related to the Dorian mode because that is the chord that results from building a diatonic 7th chord up from the root of the Dorian mode. The numbers above the scales refer to the parallel major scales and the alterations needed to get to the mode. For instance, if you lower the the 3rd and 7th degrees of a D Major scale (♭3 and ♭7) you will have a D Dorian mode.

57

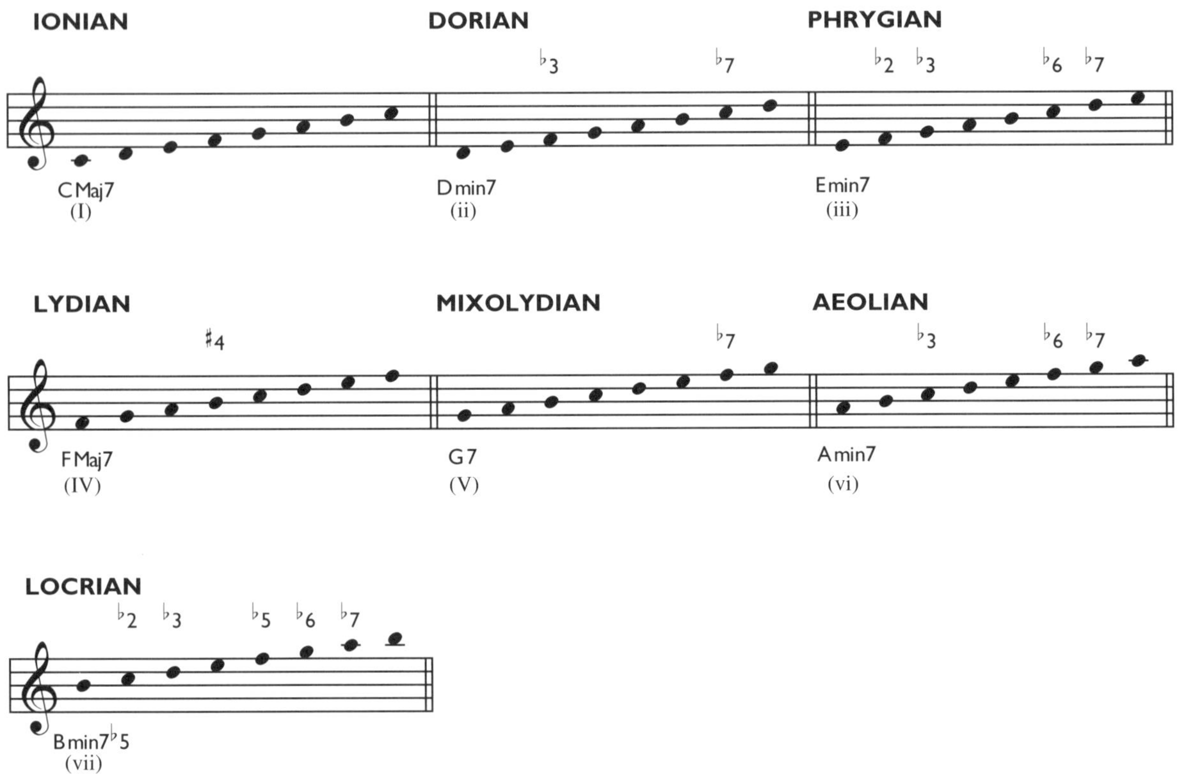

TWO VIEWS OF THE MODES

As you have just learned, every mode can be viewed in one of two ways:

The relative view—Every mode can be viewed as being a scale that occurs when you play a major scale starting and ending on a note other than the root. The Dorian mode occurs when playing a major scale starting and ending on the 2nd degree. The Mixolydian mode starts when playing a major scale starting and ending on the 5th degree.

The parallel view—Every mode has a formula of it's own. The Dorian mode is what happens when you take any major scale and lower the 3rd (♭3) and 7th (♭7) degrees. The Mixolydian mode is what happens when you take any major scale and lower the 7th (♭7) degree.

To prepare for the next two pieces—*A Dorian Mood* in the Dorian mode and *All Mixed Up* in the Mixolydian mode—let's take a look at the Dorian and Mixolydian modes from a parallel point of view.

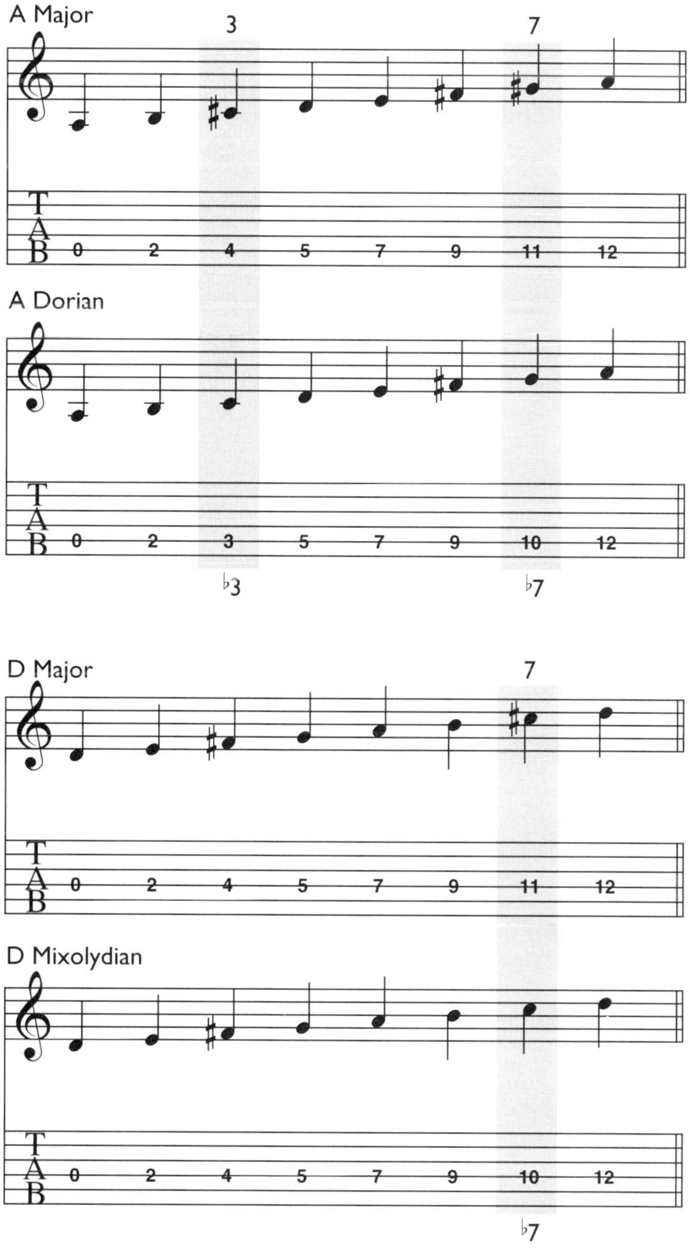

A DORIAN MOOD

Track 63

ALL MIXED UP

Track 64

CHAPTER 11

Counterpoint

By now you have learned many fingerstyle pieces—those provided in this book and hopefully, those in *Beginning Fingerstyle Guitar*. Also, you have probably learned other pieces from other sources. Maybe you have learned some of the pieces that initially inspired you to play fingerstyle guitar. Fantastic!

This chapter, and the one following on arranging, are about getting your own creative juices flowing. If you are a naturally creative person, you have already tried composing or arranging fingerstyle pieces. That's great, because mostly we learn by doing. The materials discussed in this chapter are meant to help you along in that process.

THREE KINDS OF MOVEMENT

As you know by now, one of the coolest things about fingerstyle guitar is the ability to play more than one part. this means *counterpoint* is available to us as a tool. Counterpoint refers to playing two or more melodies (voices) at the same time. This often referred to as *contrapuntal* playing. There are three ways that moving lines relate in counterpoint:

1. Similar motion—The voices move in the same direction.
2. Oblique motion—One voice moves and the other doesn't.
3. Contrasting motion—The voices move in opposite directions.

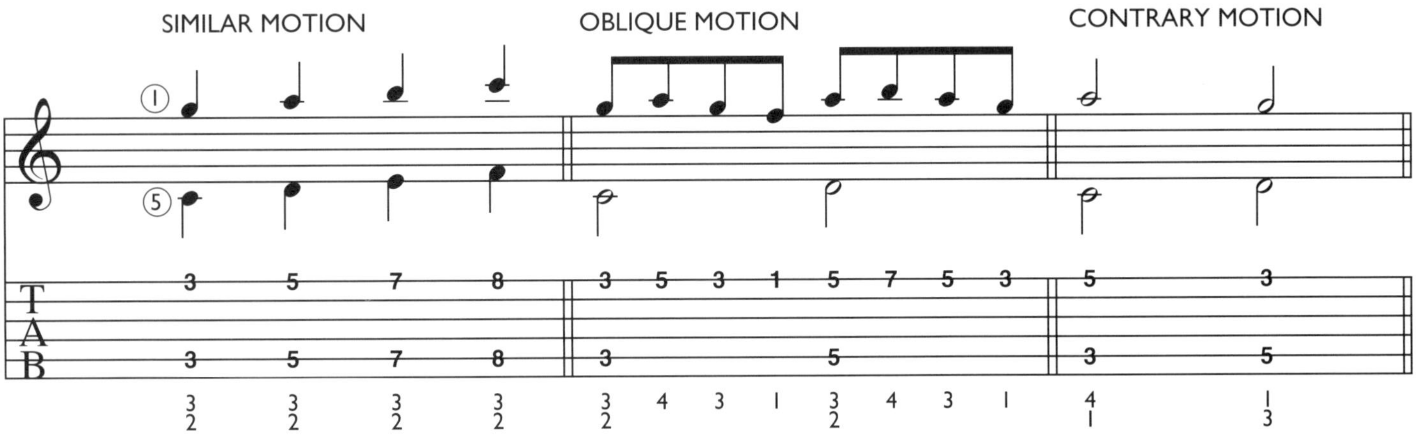

Over the next several pages we will take a look at these three types of contrapuntal movement applied to the guitar. We are going to be using the C Major scale as grist for our mill, so let's check it out.

58

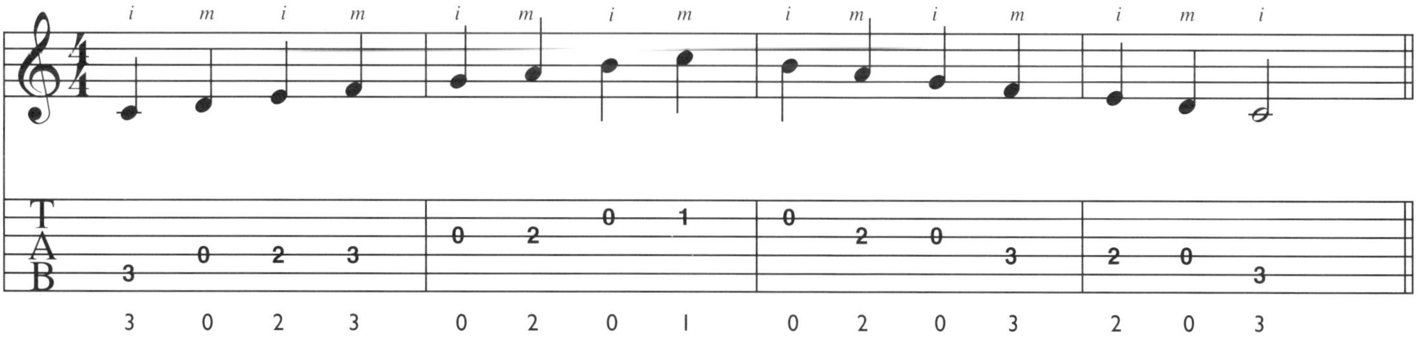

Here's the scale again, this time going over all six strings in the first position. Make sure you have thoroughly familiarized yourself with this material before going on.

59

Example 60 is a good demonstration of basic counterpoint using oblique motion. The low voice, or bass, moves very slowly through the C Major scale, starting on C on the 3rd fret of the 5th string and moving down to the low E on the open 6th string. The high voice, or *treble*, moves more quickly up and down through the scale.

60

Track 65

Example 61 uses a combination of oblique and similar motion. The first measure, for instance, uses oblique motion—the bass stays still while the treble moves up and down. But the movement from the first measure into the the second is similar motion—the treble descends to C as the bass descends to B. Notice that the B and C are *dissonant* (they clash). This is OK because the treble resolves up to the D, which is *consonant* (harmonious) with the B on the very next eighth note.

61

Track 66

The alternating bass in Example 62 results in an ongoing mixture of similar and contrasting motion.

62

Track 67

This piece is in the key of A Minor, which is the relative minor key of C Major (*Beginning Fingerstyle Guitar*, page 35). The only different note in A Minor is the G♯. Notice how the bass and treble voices relate, and see if you can identify the different kinds of counterpoint, the kind of bass line being used, etc. Have fun and swing those eighths!

THE CAT'S MEOW

Track 68

CHAPTER 12

Arranging

Arranging has always been a big part of fingerstyle guitar playing. In fact, it is fair to say that plucked string instruments did not enter the realm of solo instrumental playing until people starting doing plucked arrangements. Believe it or not, it all started back in the 15th century. It was then that the *lute* players (a lute is a sister intrument to the guitar with a bowl shaped body and an angled peg head) started arranging choral works by famous composers for their instrument. Not long after, guitar players and other pluckers got the idea—"Hey! We can play something other than dance tunes. Cool!"

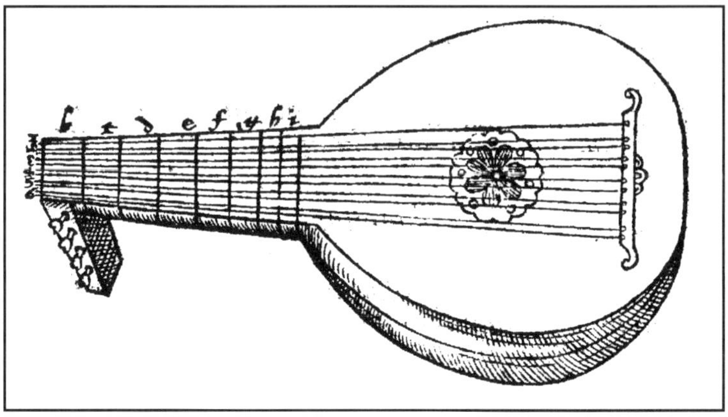

A Lute

Now, while the lute's day has past, arranging for plucked strings is a great guitar tradition. For some players, such as Chet Atkins, it's a specialty. Many other players, such as Ed Gerhard, Martin Simpson and Pierre Bensusan include arrangements of traditional tunes in their repertoire.

At it's heart, arranging is simply the placing of a melody in a new context. The melody can be left essentially untouched, but the harmony or feel may be changed. The melody itself can be altered or used as a basis for creating a new melody. Almost any musical element, from rhythm to time signature to the bass line—anything you can think of—is fair game to the arranger.

In this book, we will deal with basic arranging. We will use the timeless melody of Scarborough Fair to develop the ideas. First, we'll learn the traditional melody. Then we will begin to add various elements to the tune, finally arriving at a full-blown arrangement. Dig in!

PHOTO BY EVE EDELSTEIN/COURTESY OF VIRTUE PRODUCTIONS

Ed Gerhard came on the national scene in the late 1980s. Not only is he a fine player and composer, he is a brilliant arranger. Check out his heart-wrenching rendition of The Water is Wide, *which he performs in the* Fingerstyle Summit *video.*

Since it is important to the arranger to be aware of the harmony, the chord symbols are included in the music.

SCARBOROUGH FAIR—MELODY

Track 69

Now that you have the melody in your ears, let's add a simple bass part. The best way to begin building your bass part is to simply play the roots of the chords. Just one bass note per measure. It won't sound fancy, but it will sound right.

SCARBOROUGH FAIR—MELODY AND SLOW BASS

Track 70

It's time to add a little window dressing to your arrangement. For now, stay with just the two voices, melody and bass. Develop your bass line using the devices you know, such as arpeggios and walking bass. Study the chords in your arrangement and find ways to arpeggiate them on the bass strings. When there is a long note in the melody, such as a half note, move your bass line through an arpeggio. While the melody is moving, do less in the bass. Learn the sample arrangement below bass line first. Now that both the bass and melody are moving, there will be new challenges for the left hand. Practice small sections, slowly, before putting it all together.

SCARBOROUGH FAIR—MELODY AND QUICKER BASS

Track 71

If you like, you can call your arrangement done. Some of the most brilliant arrangements are the most simple. Listen to Martin Simpson's arrangement of *Lord Jamie Douglas* on his "Cool and Unusual" CD. Very few notes can make a powerful statement.

But, assuming you need more, try adding a third, middle voice to your arrangement. Just use other notes from the chords that work well with your melody and bass line. You may have to alter a fingering or two to make it work.

SCARBOROUGH FAIR—IN THREE VOICES

Track 72

melody to play with it. These are often called *counter melodies*. Let's put the information from Chapter 11 to work in our arrangement of *Scarborough Fair*. In this case, we have added counter melodies below the main tune, in both the bass and the middle parts. In the first six measures, the counterpoint is mostly two-voiced—treble and bass. In measures seven through eleven, a third voice is added in the middle. Try playing each voice separately before putting them together.

SCARBOROUGH FAIR—CONTRAPUNTAL

Track 73

If you haven't done so already, start creating your own arrangements of tunes you love. This topic will be taken up again in *Mastering Fingerstyle Guitar*, where we will continue to experiment with *Scarborough Fair*. Let's see how far you can develop this skill until then.

EXPLORING THE STYLES

Enjoy playing all of these tunes, each in another great style. Have fun!

DANCING DREAMS

Track 74

In the Style of John Fahey

Track 75

RISE AND SHINE

In the Style of Leo Kottke

Notice that there are no plucked notes in this piece—all the notes in the left hand part are hammered-on or pulled-off. Also note the *slap harmonics* in the right hand part (R.H.). These are executed by slapping directly over the indicated fret with the thumb side of your *i* finger. If you hit just the right spot hard enough, harmonics will sound. A *right hand tap* (R.H. Tap) is done by hammering the indicated fret quite hard with *i* or *m*, sounding the note without plucking, as in a hammer-on. Modern techniques such as this are covered thoroughly in *Mastering Fingerstyle Guitar*.

L.H. = Left Hand
R.H. = Right Hand

THE ROAD TO YOU

Track 76

In the Style of Michael Hedges

Tune to: DADGBE

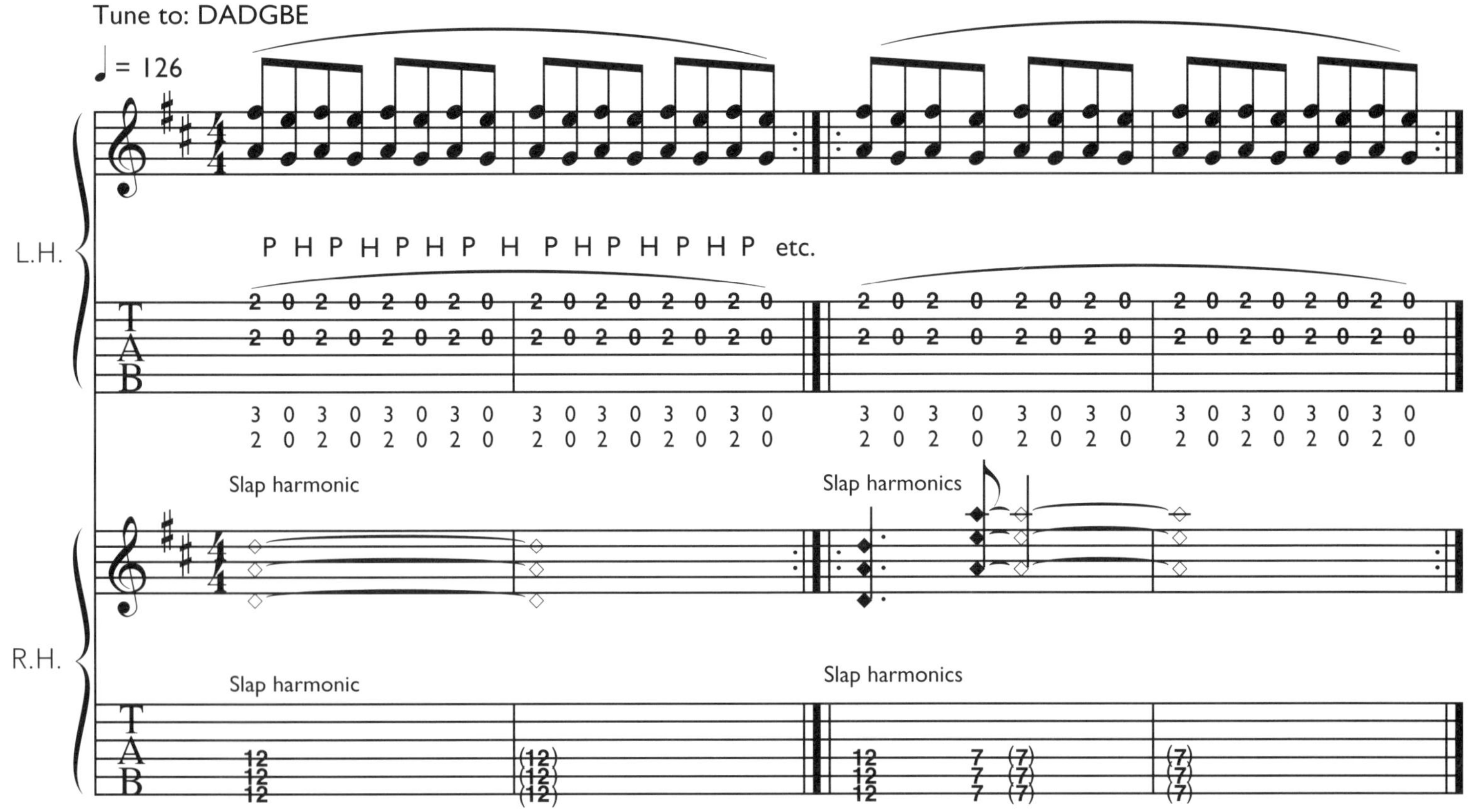

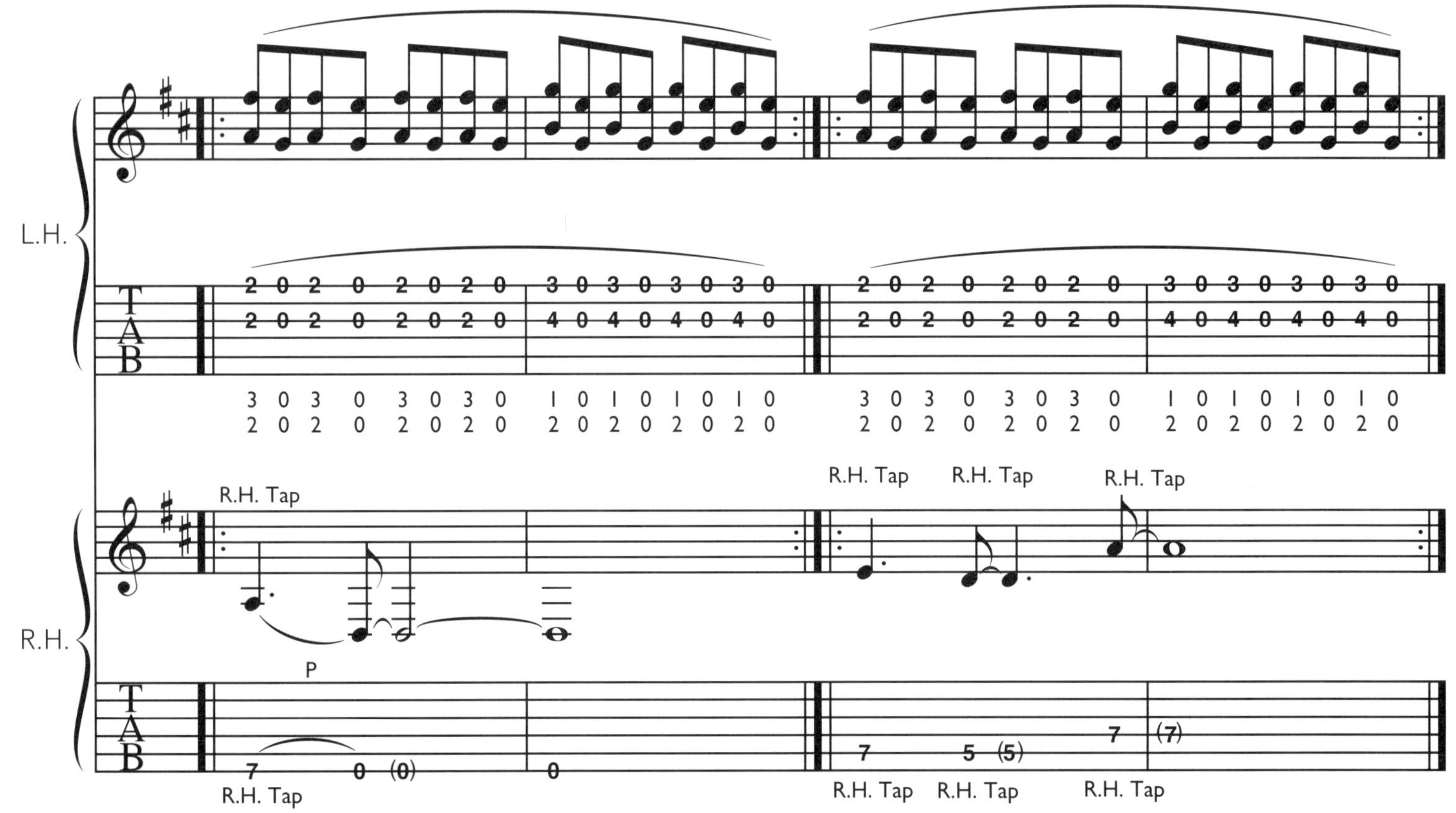

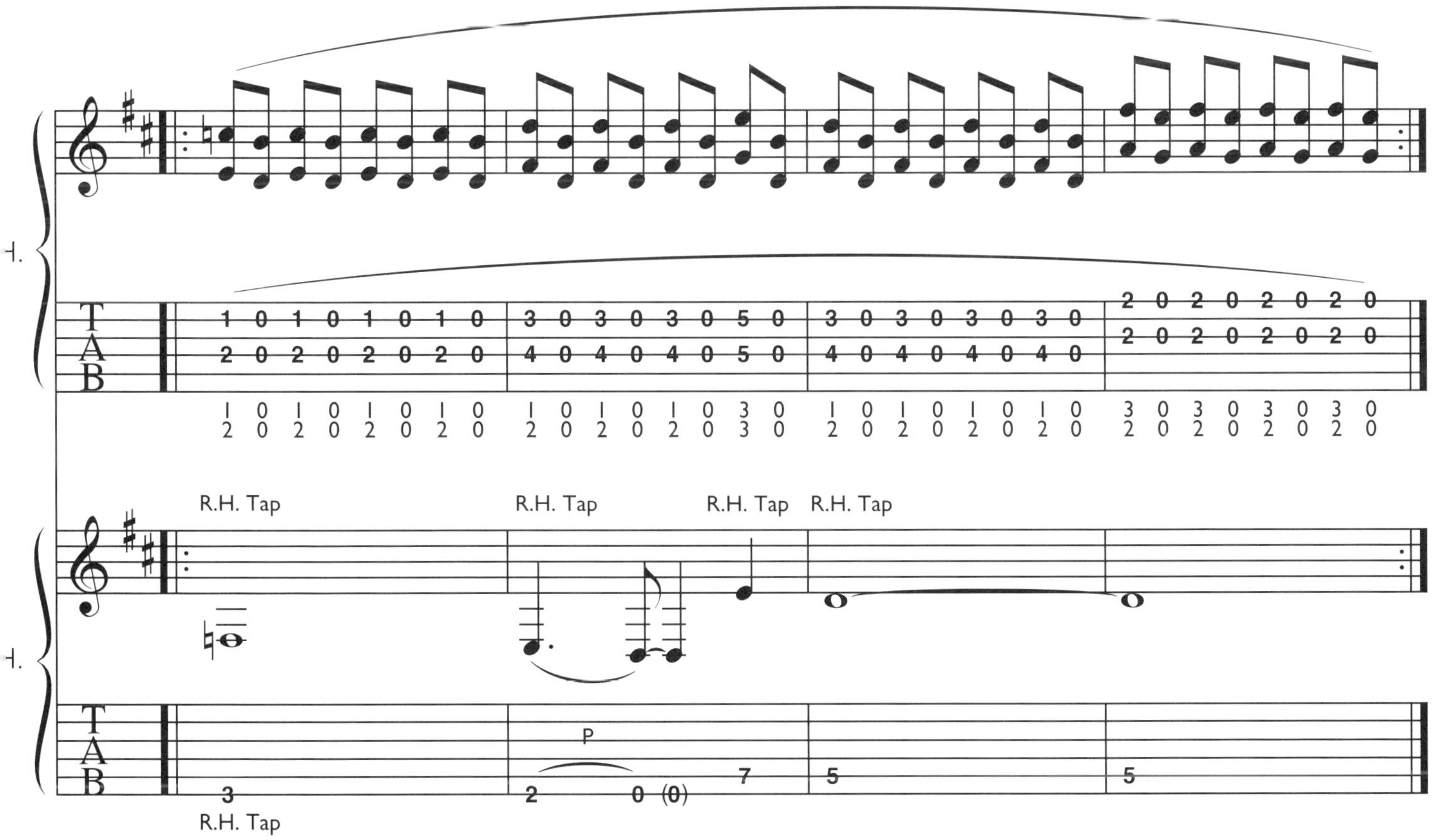
R.H. Tap
R.H. Tap
R.H. Tap
R.H. Tap
P
R.H. Tap

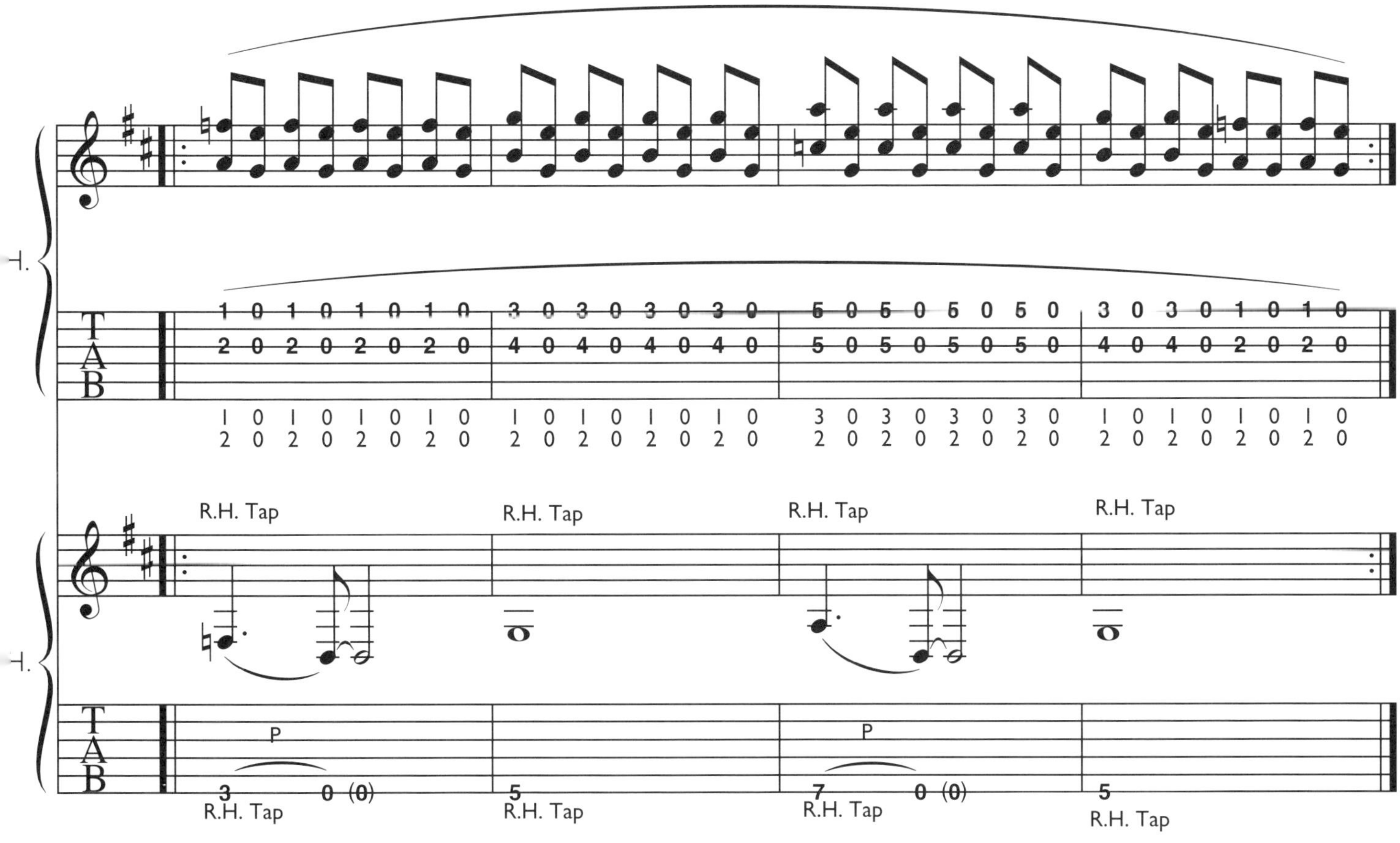
R.H. Tap
R.H. Tap
R.H. Tap
R.H. Tap
P
P
R.H. Tap
R.H. Tap
R.H. Tap
R.H. Tap

THANKS TO JOSIE

IN THE STYLE OF ADRIAN LEGG

SMASH THE WINDOWS

Track 78

AN IRISH TUNE

SI BEAG SI MOR

Track 79

AN IRISH CLASSIC BY O'CAROLAN

HOT PEPPER BLUES

Track 80

FINGERSTYLE BLUES

Track 81

HANGIN' AROUND

AFTER DARK

Track 84

FINGERSTYLE BLUES

THE REVEREND'S RAG

Track 83

Fingerstyle Blues in the Style of Rev. Gary Davis

AFTERWORD

Congratulations. You have traveled quite a distance since beginning your explorations of fingerstyle guitar. We hope the process of learning has been fulfilling and joyful, and that you will continue to challenge yourself by moving on to *Mastering Fingerstyle Guitar*.

By now, you have mastered many fingerstyle patterns and learned lots of tunes. You have picked-up some important standard techniques, such as hammer-ons, pull-offs, slides, vibrato, barres, harmonics and bends, and even a couple of less traditional techniques such as slap harmonics and right-hand tapping. You have studied the basics of counterpoint and arranging. It is fair to say that you have a good grasp of the basic possibilities available to fingerstyle guitarists.

The serious student is bound to be wondering what to do next, and the obvious answer is to continue your studies with *Mastering Fingerstyle Guitar*. That is only a small part of the answer, however.

In terms of technical development, you have only just begun. Practically speaking, there is virtually no limit to what a player can accomplish technically. The only real limit is your imagination. The only thing that can limit your imagination is a lack of curiosity. Listen to what other artists, from all styles of music, have done on the guitar. For instance, listen to the incredible speed of jazz guitarist Tal Farlow, fusion player Al Di Meola or classical guitarists such as John Williams. Observe the sheer power of the blues master B.B. King's vibrato, or the absolute clarity and evenness of classical virtuoso, Manuel Barrueco. Look at what Eddie Van Halen accomplishes with tapping. If you only listen to fingerstyle players—even though this is an incredibly diverse group—you will be missing a lot. We have something to learn from every guitarist.

This is true of your expressive and creative powers, too. The more you have heard, the more you can imagine. Yes, you have looked into the expressive devices of artists such Pierre Bensusan and Michael Hedges, but that is just the beginning. Consider the emotional power of Yehudi Menuhen's violin playing, or the manipulations of time (*rubato*) used by great jazz or classical pianists. Investigate the contrapuntal mastery of J. S. Bach, the free improvisations of John Coltrane and the songwriting of the Beatles. Your ability to create interesting, moving and satisfying music will depend upon how many different types of music you have heard and how well you have listened.

Your "book learning" is important, too. While some successful musicians claim a limited knowledge of music, there is nothing to gain by purposefully choosing to remain uninformed. There are great books on theory (such as *Theory for the Contemporary Guitarist* by Guy Capuzzo), technique (take a look at *Pumping Nylon* by Scott Tennant) and ear-training (check out *Learn How to Transcribe for Guitar* by Tobias Hurwitz). Your local colleges may offer classes on music theory and history that you can take. While you should never let schooling get in the way of a good education, remember that Michael Hedges, one of our most creative fingerstylists, had a college degree in classical composition!

The world of music is so vast that a lifetime of listening and exploration is not enough to experience it all. This is why music is such a wonderful pursuit. The more you learn, the more you will realize there is left to learn. We wish you a long and satisfying musical journey, and much happiness along the way.

APPENDIX

Open Chords

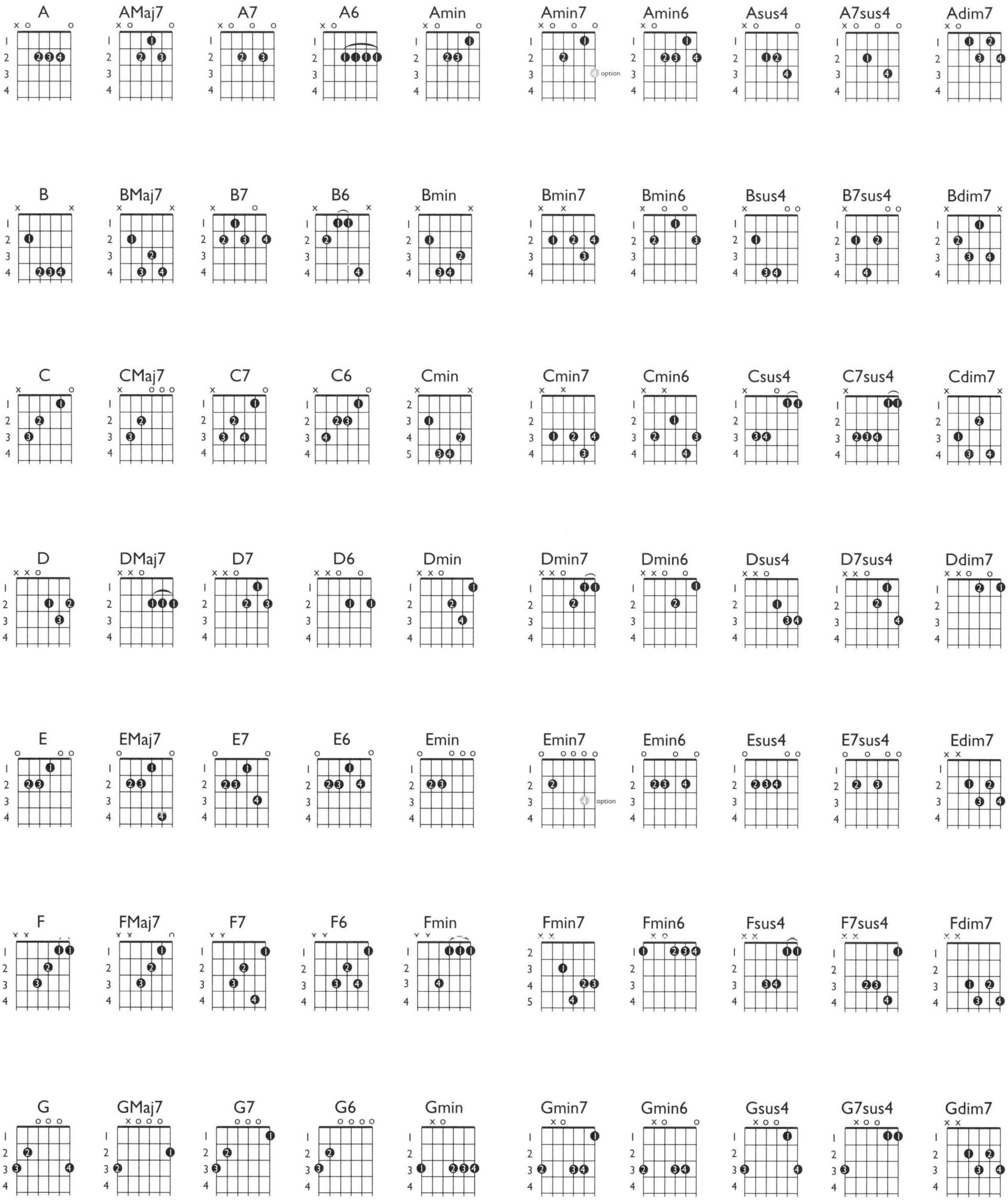

IF YOU ENJOYED THIS BOOK, YOU'LL LOVE OUR SCHOOL

NATIONAL GUITAR SUMMER WORKSHOP

- Study music in an intensive and friendly environment.
- Locations in Connecticut, California, Canada, Orlando, Austin, and Nashville.
- Students of all ages and levels enjoy learning from visiting artists and an outstanding professional faculty in week-long summer sessions.
- Classes are available for the beginner through the professional player.
- Design a course of study that fits your needs.

ROCK-BLUES-JAZZ-CLASSICA
ACOUSTIC-COUNTRY-FUNK-FUSIO
ALTERNATIVE-BASS-GUITAR-REPAI
KEYBOARDS-SONGWRITING-DRUMS-VOIC

n.g.s.w

BOX 222
LAKESIDE, CT., 06758
1-800-234-6479

CALL OR WRITE FOR YOUR FREE BROCHURE